LAND

A Newfoundland & Labrador
Literature Anthology

Eric Norman
Stanley Sparkes
June Warr

BREAKWATER

Canadian Cataloguing in Publication Data

Main entry under title:
Landings: Newfoundland literature anthology

ISBN 0-919519-74-1

1. Canadian literature (English) — Newfoundland.*
2. Canadian literature (English) — 20th century.*

I. Norman, Eric.

PS8255.N49L35 1984   C810'.8'09718 ·   C84-099166-5
PR9198.2.N492L35 1984

Illustrations by Don Wright

ACKNOWLEDGEMENTS

"Eight-Year Old" by Geraldine Rubia. Reprinted by permission of the author.

"The Outboard Motor" reprinted from *My Newfoundland* by A.R. Scammell, published by Harvest House of Montreal, 1966.

"What A Charm, What A Racket" by Ray Guy, first appeared in *The Evening Telegram*. Reprinted by permission of the author.

"The Wreck of the *Florizel*," excerpt from *A Winter's Tale* by Cassie Brown. Copyright ©1976 by Cassie Brown. Reprinted by permission of Doubleday and Company, Inc.

"Brigus, Newfoundland" reprinted from *North By East* by Rockwell Kent, published by copyright ©1978 Wesleyan University Press.

"Newfoundland Disaster (1914) (after Cassie Brown)" from *After The Locusts* by Enos Watts, Breakwater Books Ltd., 1974. Reprinted by permission of the author.

"The Soul of a Newfoundlander" by Cyril Poole. Reprinted from *In Search of the Newfoundland Soul*, Harry Cuff Publications Ltd., 1983.

"This Dear and Fine Country – Spina Sanctus" by Ray Guy first appeared in *The Evening Telegram*. Reprinted by permission of the author.

"Abandoned Outport" by Tom Dawe. Reprinted from *Island Spell*, Harry Cuff Publications Ltd., 1981.

"Transition" by Harold Horwood, from *Beyond the Road*, first published by Macmillan of Canada. Reprinted by permission of the author.

"Moving Day" by Helen Porter. Reprinted from *Baffles of Wind and Tide*, edited by Fraser and Rose, Breakwater Books Ltd., 1974. Reprinted by permission of the author.

"Leave-Taking" by Geraldine Rubia. Reprinted from *East of Canada*, edited by Fraser, Rose and Stewart, Breakwater Books Ltd., 1977. Reprinted by permission of the author.

"St. Leonard's Revisited" reprinted from *Once When I Was Drowning* by Al Pittman, Breakwater Books Ltd., 1978.

"West Moon Song" by Pat Byrne. Copyright © Music and Lyrics, P.A. Byrne (CAPAC). Arrangement by Sheila Brown.

"This Morning I Sat" by Rosalie Fowler. Reprinted from *31 Newfoundland Poets*, edited by Fowler and Pittman, Breakwater Books Ltd., 1979. Reprinted by permission of the author.

"Didymus on Saturday" from "A Suite for Easter" by David Elliott. Reprinted from *31 Newfoundland Poets*, edited by Fowler and Pittman, 1979. (First appeared in Newfoundland Quarterly, 1954) Reprinted by permission of the author.

"Silver Birches" by R.A. Parsons. Reprinted from *CurtainCall*, Harry Cuff Publications Ltd.

"Essence of Wild Newfunlan" by Kevin Major. Reprinted by permission of the author.

"Schoonerman" by Gregory Power. Reprinted by permission of the author.

"Varick Frissell" by Irving Fogwill. Reprinted from *A Short Distance Only*, Harry Cuff Publications Ltd.

"Shadows: Jamie's Last Ride" by Enos Watts. Previously published in *The Antigonish Review* (No. 45, Spring, 1981) and *CV-II* (Vol. 6, No. 3, Spring, 1982).

"Two Men Went Out" by Harold Paddock. Reprinted from *Tung Tide*, Harry Cuff Publications Ltd., 1981.

"A Newfoundland Garden" by Percy Janes. Reprinted from *Light and Dark*, Harry Cuff Publications Ltd., 1980.

"Bogwood" by Gregory Power. Reprinted by permission of the author.

"Lines for My Grandfather Long Gone" reprinted from *Once When I Was Drowning* by Al Pittman, Breakwater Books Ltd., 1978.

"Alces the Moose" by Donald Dodds. Reprinted from *Wild Captives*, Macmillan (Canada) and St. Martin's Press, 1965. Reprinted by permission of the author.

"The Migrating Caribou" reprinted from *A Woman's Way Through Unknown Labrador* by Mina Hubbard, Breakwater Books Ltd., 1983.

"The Miracle of the Caplin" by Harold Horwood. Reprinted from *Newfoundland* by permission of Macmillan of Canada, a Division of Gage Publishing Limited, 1969.

"Notes to No One" by Al Pittman from *Through One More Window*, Breakwater Books Ltd., 1974.

Contents

UNIT 1

A Part of All That We Have Met

A Part Of All That We Have Met

Tennyson's Ulysses, in explaining his great urge to find adventure, states that the experience of the past largely determines the characteristics, motivations and behaviours of people in the present. For people living near the edge of the ocean for four hundred years the explanation holds some validity. We Newfoundlanders have become "sea people" regardless of where we live. We are influenced by the sea whether we live inland or by the landwash. We have an oceanic, marine perspective in much of our dealings with life experiences. To illustrate, we have more words to name bodies of water than most people living elsewhere: bay, harbor, cove, sound, run, tickle, and gut. And there are others which you could add to the list. We also speak of flag masts rather than poles, we sometimes cruise rather than ride in a vehicle, and we have bridges on our houses. A little thought will reward you with many other everyday examples of our salt-water orientation. Many of our writers express this perspective in their work. Some do it to add color or character, others do it to present a specific and special picture of people shaped by and reacting to their environment. This unit has a number of selections which are illustrative. It opens with a work by Norman Duncan, which, when written many years ago, was all too close to reality. The unit closes with an essay by Dr. Poole who makes many references to Duncan's work as he expounds the importance of our marine environment in the development of what he calls "the Newfoundland soul". Rockwell Kent offers an outsider's view of the impact of a great tragedy on the people of a Newfoundland outport, and illustrates how the people react to the adversity. Death is a part of life and molds the lives of the living. In a somewhat similar way, but in a manner not really spelled out for us, the child in Rubia's poem will become "a part of all" that he will meet. The short piece by Scammell is crafted to place full emphasis on an adult character typical of the marine environment. For a detailed account of the impact of sounds and sights and smells on the developing child we have a vivid essay by Ray Guy, who, we might say, is offering us "soul food". The philosophy which is spawned by a life of danger and hardship near and on the ocean is clearly outlined in Cassie Brown's rendering of the wrecking of a passenger liner; and Enos Watts offers a poet's response to the great tragedy of the ice fields in 1914. As you enjoy these selections try to determine to some extent how you have become a part of all that you have met.

"Fatalism is not a conviction that our dory will fail to make it, but a sense that it is beyond one's control whether she makes it or not. Fatalism permits of struggle and battle even though the outcome rests with the gods." — Poole

In this short story by Norman Duncan we witness such a struggle. Notice particularly how Duncan uses dialect in the narrative parts and poignant diction in the descriptive sections to arouse the reader's empathy for Solomon and Priscilla. The skillful treatment of time helps the plot unfold so that we experience a sensation of having lived through it all with the people in the story. These were harsh times in a harsh land. Nature's savage battle against man dominates, yet the indomitable spirit of man rises again and again.

The Days of Solomon Stride

How the wilderness, savage and remote, yields to the strength of men! A generation strips it of tree and rock, a generation tames it and tills it, a generation passes into the evening shadows as into rest in a garden, and thereafter the children of that place possess it in peace and plenty, through succeeding generations, without end, and shall to the end of the world. But the sea is tameless: as it was in the beginning, it is now, and shall ever be — mighty, savage, dread, infinitely treacherous and hateful, yielding only that which is wrested from it, snarling, raging, snatching lives, spoiling souls of their graces. The tiller of the soil sows in peace, and in a yellow, hazy peace he reaps; he passes his hand over a field, and, lo, in good season he gathers a harvest, for the earth rejoices to serve him. The deep is not thus subdued; the toiler of the sea — the Newfoundlander of the upper shore — is born to conflict, ceaseless and deadly, and, in the dawn of all the days, he puts forth anew to wage it, as his father did, and his father's father, and as his children must, and his children's children, to the last of them; nor from day to day can he foresee the issue, nor from season to season foretell the worth of the spoil, which is what chance allows. Thus laboriously, precariously, he slips through life: he follows hope through the toilsome years; and past summers are a black regret and bitterness to him, but summers to come are all rosy with new promise.

Long ago, when young Luke Dart, the Boot Bay trader, was ambitious for Shore patronage, he said to Solomon Stride, of Ragged Harbour, a punt fisherman: "Solomon b'y, an' you be willin', I'll trust you with twine for a cod-trap. An you trade with me, b'y, I'll trade with you, come good times or bad." Solomon was young and lusty, a mighty youth in bone and seasoned muscle, lunged like a blast furnace, courageous and finely sanguine. Said he: "An you trust me with twine for a trap, skipper,

3

I'll deal fair by you, come good times or bad. I'll pay for un, skipper, with the first fish I cotches." Said Luke Dart: "When I trust, b'y, I trust. You pays for un when you can." It was a compact, so at the end of the season Solomon builded a cottage under the Man-o'-War, Broad Cove way, and married a maid of the place. In five months of that winter he made the trap, every net of it, leader and all, with his own hands, that he might know that the work was good, to the last knot and splice. In the spring he put up the stage and the flake, and made the skiff; which done, he waited for a sign of fish. When the tempered days came he hung the net on the horse, where it could be seen from the threshold of the cottage. In the evenings he sat with Priscilla on the bench at the door, and dreamed great dreams, while the red sun went down in the sea, and the shadows crept out of the wilderness.

"Woman, dear," said this young Solomon Stride, with a slap of his great thigh, " 'twill be a gran' season for fish this year."

"Sure, b'y," said Priscilla, tenderly: " 'twill be a gran' season for fish."

"Ay," Solomon sighed, " 'twill that — this year."

The gloaming shadows gathered over the harbour water, and hung, sullenly, between the great rocks rising all roundabout.

" 'Tis handy t' three hundred an' fifty dollars I owes Luke Dart for the twine," muses Solomon.

" 'Tis a hape o' money t' owe," said Priscilla.

"Hut!" growled Solomon, deep in his chest. " 'Tis like nothin'."

" 'Tis not much," said Priscilla, smiling, "when you has a trap."

Dusk and a clammy mist chased the glory from the hills; the rocks turned black, and a wind, black and cold, swept out of the wilderness and ran to sea.

"Us'll pay un all up this year," said Solomon. "Oh," he added loftily, " 'twill be easy. 'Tis t' be a gran' season."

"Sure!" said she, echoing his confidence.

Night filled the cloudy heavens overhead. It drove the flush of pink in upon the sun, and, following fast and overwhelmingly, thrust the flaring red and gold over the rim of the sea; and it was dark.

"Us'll pay un for a trap, dear," chuckled Solomon, "an have enough left over t' buy a — "

"Oh," she cried, with an ecstatic gasp, "a sewin' machane!"

"Iss," he roared. "Sure, girl!"

But in the beginning of that season when the first fish ran in for the caplin, and the nets were set out, the ice was still hanging off shore, drifting vagrantly with the wind; and there came a gale in the night, springing from the northeast — a great, vicious wind, which gathered the ice in a pack and drove it swiftly in upon the land. Solomon Stride put off in a punt, in a sea tossing and white, to loose the trap from its moorings. Three times, while the pack swept nearer, crunching and horribly groaning, as though lashed to cruel speed by the gale, the wind beat him back through the tickle; and, upon the fourth essay, when his strength was breaking, the ice ran over the place where the trap was, and chased the punt into the harbour, frothing upon its flank. When, three days thereafter, a west wind carried the ice to sea, Solomon dragged the trap from the bottom. Great holes were bruised in the nets, head rope and span line were ground to pulp, the anchors were

4

lost. Thirty-seven days and nights it took to make the nets whole again, and in that time the great spring run of cod passed by. So, in the next spring, Solomon was deeper in the debt of sympathetic Luke Dart — for the new twine and for the winter's food he had eaten; but, of an evening, when he sat on the bench with Priscilla, he looked through the gloaming shadows gathered over the harbour water and hanging between the great rocks, to the golden summer approaching, and dreamed gloriously of the fish he would catch in his trap.

"Priscilla, dear," said Solomon Stride, slapping his iron thigh, "they be a fine sign o'fish down the coast. 'Twill be a gran' season, I'm thinkin'."

; "Sure, b'y," Priscilla agreed; " 'twill be a gran' cotch o' fish you'll have this year."

Dusk and the mist touched the hills, and, in the dreamful silence, their glory faded; the rocks turned black, and the wind from the wilderness ruffled the water beyond the flake.

"Us'll pay Luke Dart this year, I tells you," said Solomon, like a boastful boy. "Us'll pay un twice over."

" 'Twill be fine t' have the machane," said she, with shining eyes.

"An' the calico t'use un on," said he.

And so, while the night spread overhead, these two simple folk feasted upon all the sweets of life; and all that they desired they possessed, as fast as fancy could form wishes, just as though the bench were a bit of magic furniture to bring dreams true — until the night, advancing, thrust the red and gold of the sunset clouds over the rim of the sea, and it was dark.

"Leave us goa in," said Priscilla.

"This year," said Solomon, rising, "I be goain' t' cotch three hundred quintals o' fish. Sure, I be — this year."

" 'Twill be fine," said she.

It chanced in that year that the fish failed utterly; hence, in the winter following, Ragged Harbour fell upon days of distress; and three old women and one old man starved to death — and five children, of whom one was the infant son of Solomon Stride. Neither in that season, nor in any one of the thirteen years coming after did this man catch three hundred quintals of cod in his trap. In pure might of body — in plenitude and quality of strength — in the full, eager power of brawn — he was great as the men of any time, a towering glory to the whole race, here hidden; but he could not catch three hundred quintals of cod. In spirit — in patience, hope, courage, and the fine will for toil — he was great; but, good season or bad, he could not catch three hundred quintals of cod. He met night, cold, fog, wind, and the fury of waves, in their craft, in their swift assault, in their slow, crushing descent; but all the cod he could wrest from the sea, being given into the hands of Luke Dart, an honest man, yielded only sufficient provision of food and clothing for himself and Priscilla — only enough to keep their bodies warm and still the crying of their stomachs. Thus, while the nets of the trap rotted, and Solomon came near to middle age, the debt swung from seven hundred dollars to seven, and back to seventy-three, which it was on an evening in spring when he sat with Priscilla on the sunken bench at the door, and dreamed great dreams, as he watched the shadows gather over the harbour water and sullenly hang between the great rocks, rising all roundabout.

"I wonder, b'y," said Priscilla, "if 'twill be a good season — this year."

"Oh, sure!" exclaimed Solomon. "Sure!" ;   "D'ye think it, b'y?" wistfully.

"Woman," said he, impressively, "Us'll cotch a hape o' fish in the trap this year. They be millions o' fish t' the say," he went on excitedly; "millions o' fish t' the say. They be there, woman. 'Tis oan'y for us t' take un out. I be goain' t' work hard this year."

"You be a great warker, Solomon," said she: "my, but you be!"

Priscilla smiled, and Solomon smiled; and it was as though all the labour and peril of the season were past, and the stage were full to the roof with salt cod. In the happiness of this dream they smiled again, and turned their eyes to the hills, from which the glory of purple and yellow was departing to make way for the misty dusk.

* * *

In thirty years after that time Solomon Stride put to sea ten thousand times. Ten thousand times he passed through the tickle rocks to the free, heaving deep for salmon and cod, thereto compelled by the inland waste, which contributes nothing to the sustenance of the men of that coast. Hunger, lurking in the shadows of days to come, inexorably drove him into the chances of the conflict. Perforce he matched himself ten thousand times against the restless might of the sea, immeasurable and unrestrained, surviving the gamut of its moods because he was great in strength, fearlessness, and cunning. He weathered four hundred gales, from the grey gusts which come down between Quid Nunc and the Man-o'-War, leaping upon the fleet, to the summer tempests, swift and black, and the first blizzards of winter. He was wrecked off the Mull, off the Three Poor Sisters, on the Pancake Rock, and again off the Mull. Seven times he was swept out to sea by the offshore wind. Eighteen times he was frozen to the seat of his punt; and of these, eight times his feet were frozen, and thrice his festered right hand. All this he suffered, and more, of which I may set down six separate periods of starvation, in which thirty-eight men, women, and children died, — all this, with all the toil, cold, despair, loneliness, hunger, peril, and disappointment therein contained. And so he came down to old age — with a bent back, shrunken arms, and filmy eyes — old Solomon Stride, now prey for the young sea. But, of an evening in spring, he sat with Priscilla on the sunken bench at the door, and talked hopefully of the fish he would catch from his punt.

"Priscilla, dear," said he, rubbing his hand over his weazened thigh, "I be thinkin' us punt fishermen'll have a — "

Twenty-one years longer old Solomon Stride fished out of Ragged Harbour. He put to sea five thousand times more, weathered two hundred more gales, survived five more famines — all in the toil for salmon and cod. He was a punt fisherman again, was old Solomon; for the nets of the trap had rotted, had been renewed six times, strand by strand, and had rotted at last beyond repair. What with the weather he dared not pit his failing strength against, the return of fish to Luke Dart fell off from year to year;

6

but, as Solomon said to Luke, "livin' expenses kep' up wonderful," notwithstanding.

"I be so used t' luxuries," he went on, running his hand through his long grey hair, "that 'twould be hard t' come down t' common livin'. Sure 'tis sugar I wants a t' me tea — not black-strap. 'Tis what I l'arned," he added proudly, "when I were a trap fisherman."

" 'Tis all right, Solomon," said Luke. "Many's the quintal o' fish you traded with me."

"Sure," Solomon chuckled; " 'twould take a year t' count un."

In course of time it came to the end of Solomon's last season — those days of it when, as the folk of the coast say, the sea is hungry for lives — and the man was eighty-one years old, and the debt to Luke Dart had crept up to $230.80. The off-shore wind, rising suddenly, with a blizzard in its train, caught him alone on the grappling Hook grounds. He was old, very old — old and feeble and dull; the cold numbed him; the snow blinded him; the wind made sport of the strength of his arms. He was carried out to sea, rowing doggedly, thinking all the time that he was drawing nearer the harbour tickle; for it did not occur to him then that the last of eight hundred gales could be too great for him. He was carried out from the sea, where the strength of his youth had been spent, to the Deep, which had been a mystery to him all his days. That night he passed on a pan of ice, where he burned his boat, splinter by splinter, to keep warm. At dawn he lay down to die. The snow ceased, the wind changed; the ice was carried to Ragged Harbour. Eleazar Manuel spied the body of Solomon from the lookout, and put out and brought him in — revived him and took him home to Priscilla. Through the winter the old man doddered about the harbour dying of consumption. When the tempered days came — the days of balmy sunshine and cold evening winds — he came quickly to the pass of glittering visions, which, for such as die of the lung trouble, come at the end of life.

In the spring, when the *Lucky Star,* three days out from Boot Bay, put into Ragged Harbour to trade for the first catch, old Skipper Luke Dart was aboard, making his last voyage to the shore; for he was very old, and longed once more to see the rocks of all that coast before he made ready to die. When he came ashore Eleazar Manuel told him that Solomon Stride lay dying at home; so the skipper went to the cottage under the Man-o'-War to say good-bye to his old customer and friend — and there found him propped up in bed, staring at the sea.

"Skipper Luke," Solomon quavered, in deep excitement, "be you just come in, b'y?"

"Iss — but an hour gone."

The men turned their faces to the window...and gazed long and intently at the sea, which a storm cloud had turned black. Solomon dozed for a moment, and when he awoke Luke Dart was still staring dreamily out to sea.

"Skipper Luke," said Solomon, with a smile as of one in an enviable situation, " 'tis fine t' have nothin' agin you on the books when you comes t' die."

"Sure, b'y," said Luke, hesitating not at all, though he knew to a cent what was on the books against Solomon's name, " 'tis fine to be free o' debt."

"Ah," said Solomon, the smile broadening gloriously, " 'tis fine, I tells you! Twas the three hundred quintals I cotched last season that paid un all up. 'Twas a gran' cotch — last year. Ah," he sighed, " 'twas a gran' cotch o' fish."

"Iss — you be free o' debt now, b'y."

"What be the balance t' my credit, skipper? Sure I forget."

"Hem-m," the skipper coughed, pausing to form a guess which might be within Solomon's dream; then he ventured: "Fifty dollars?"

"Iss," said Solomon, "fifty an' moare, skipper. Sure you has forgot the eighty cents."

"Fifty-eighty," said the skipper, positively. " 'Tis that. I call un t' mind now. 'Tis fifty-eighty — iss, sure. Did you get a receipt for un, Solomon?"

"I doan't mind me now."

"Um-m-m — well," said the skipper. "I'll send un t' the woman on the night — an order on the *Lucky Star*."

"Fifty-eighty for the woman!" said Solomon. " 'Twill kape her off the Gov'ment for three years, an she be savin'. 'Tis fine — that!"

When the skipper had gone, Priscilla crept in, and sat at the head of the bed, holding Solomon's hand; and they were silent for a long time, while the evening approached.

"I be goain' t' die the night, dear," said Solomon at last.

"Iss, b'y," she answered: "you be goain' t' die."

Now, in that night, when the body of old Solomon Stride, a worn-out hulk, aged and wrecked in the toil of the deep, fell into the hands of Death, the sea, like a lusty youth, raged furiously in those parts. The ribs of many schooners, slimy and rotten, and the white bones of men in the off-shore depths, know of its strength in that hour — of its black, hard wrath, in gust and wave and breaker. Eternal in might and malignance is the sea! It groweth not old with the men who toil from its coasts. Generation upon the heels of generation, infinitely arising, go forth in hope against it, continuing for a space, and returning spent to the dust. They age and crumble and vanish, each in its turn, and the wretchedness of the first is the wretchedness of the last. Ay, the sea has measured the strength of the dust in old graves, and, in this day, contends with the sons of dust, whose sons will follow to the fight for a hundred generations, and thereafter, until harvests may be gathered from rocks. As it is written, the life of a man is a shadow, swiftly passing, and the days of his strength are less; but the sea shall endure in the might of youth to the wreck of the world.

Norman Duncan
(from *The Way of the Sea*)

In the early 1900's, Norman Duncan, a native of Brantford, Ontario, spent an extended period of time in Newfoundland. His love for Newfoundland and Labrador and for the people inspired him to write *The Way of the Sea* (1903), *Dr. Luke of Labrador* (1904), *Dr. Grenfell's Parish* (1905), *The Cruise of the Shining Light* and the Billy Topsail stories.

Questions

1. "Eternal in might and malignance is the sea!" How is this exclamation significant in relation to the way of life presented in the story?

2. What factors and characteristics account for Solomon's optimistic outlook in spite of great adversity?

3. Can one consider Solomon a tragic hero? Explain.

4. What are the important aspects of the roles of Priscilla and Luke Dart?

5. How does the author show that the events are indeed "beyond one's control"?

6. What techniques are used to make time pass convincingly from Solomon's youth to his old age?

Activities

1. You may find the dialect strange at first. Try this: dramatize the narrative sections. Once it takes on the aspect of a conversation between Priscilla and Solomon on their bench by their door it will become more clear to you. Use a narrator for the descriptive parts between the dialogue.

2. Invite an experienced fisherman to your class to tell about good seasons and bad seasons in the fishery.

3. Do some research on how business was conducted between merchants and fishermen in small communities along our coast during the early years of settlement.

4. Do you enjoy sketching or painting scenes? There are several descriptions in this story which might appeal to the artist — for example, "Dusk and a clammy mist chased the glory from the hills...and ran to sea". Do one or two sketches or paintings.

5. As we read this selection we feel strongly a sense of place. For an excellent parallel read "Newfoundland" by E.J. Pratt in *Theme and Image*.

When we read about the difficulties and hardships of days gone by we often wonder how it must have been for the children. But growing up is not easy even in better times. When we read a poem like "Eight-Year Old" we realize that difficulties experienced by children are timeless and universal, and are part of the experience of life. The author uses parallel structure to lend added emphasis to the main idea of the poem.

Eight-Year Old

You say you'd like to stay a child
because as you grow up
you'll have to learn
to work
to drive
to buy
to be a boy-friend
husband
father.

And then you say
a child doesn't have it easy
there are monsters
in your sleep
and you wish you had more friends
you talk to everyone
getting laughs at your joking
but they do not come to play
and Brian doesn't like you.

My son
you will grow up
don't cry
don't try so hard.

Geraldine Rubia

11

Geraldine Rubia was born in Brooklyn, New York, and now lives in Mount Pearl with her husband and two sons. Her father hails from the Goulds, her mother from Kilbride. With such variety in her background, it is not surprising that there is much variety in her writings which have been featured both locally and nationally by CBC programs. Her work can be found in such anthologies as *Newfoundland Writers 1914*, *Scrunchions*, *Baffles of Wind and Tide*, *From This Place*, *East of Canada*, *31 Newfoundland Poets*. For an indepth sampler of her poems and her recipes find a copy of her *A Poem in My Soup*.

Questions

1. What frightens the eight-year-old about growing up? What makes him cry?

2. The last four lines have particular significance. How are they related to the first two stanzas?

Activities

1. Try writing a poem of similar form. Focus on the concerns of either a twelve-year-old or a sixteen-year-old.

2. Set up a debate between three people who are over age 45 and three students who are under age 20. Topic: Be it resolved that growing up today is easier than it was in the 1940's. The over 45's debate the pro; the under 20's the con.

3. For an excellent understanding of a young girl's ambivalent feelings as she matures read "A Member of the Wedding" by Carson McCullers in *Dramatic Literature*.

4. Prayer Before Birth" by Louis MacNeish in *Man's Search for Values* presents a vivid description of what a child must face in life. Please read.

This narrative essay presents us with a situation which we know from the beginning is contrived for humour. There are many stories dealing with the "first" time some new gadget or invention came to the attention of people in the isolated outports. We might recall Ted Russell's fun with the first football to arrive in Pigeon Inlet. Here Mr. Scammell has fun by adding to the novelty of the first outboard motor, the putting on of "airs" by the owner, and the poetic justice which follows. Notice the voice of the piece, is easy and conversational.

The Outdoor Motor

"Pride an' flusteration," said Skipper Neddie, stuffing the tobacco into his pipe bowl with a huge, spade-like thumb, "are two things that makes fools of people." When the old salt started making sweeping statements on human nature, I knew he was getting wound up for a good story.

"There wuz one man I knowed," resumed the Skipper, "who had the both of them faults. Proud as a legharn rooster, an' nerviser'n a she-robin over 'er eggs. Luke Bolton his name wuz, an ornery little son-of-a-gun. Used to go fishin' in a punt be hisself. Had plenty of gall and wuz always tryin' to go one better than the rest of us. If he happened to be high-liner among the hook-and-line men any year, he'd go around proud as a peacock and brag that he used his brains and we didn't.

"One spring Luke got hold of one of those outdoor motors that hooks on the starn of a punt. The old buzzard wuz always talkin' 'bout the time he wasted, rowin' out to the grounds and back agin. One of the merchants here had this ingin come for his son, but the son died just afterwards, so his father told Luke about it. Got him all worked up over the nice, easy time he'd have, sittin' down, watchin' his punt zip along. Course Luke didn't know nothin' about runnin' the thing, but he got one of the fellers around here wot's studyin' to be an ingineer at college to larn him. Adder two weeks hard work, an' tearin' the starn off his punt and puttin' a new one on, he thought he wuz ready to leave the wharf-head.

"The second day the ingin come on the room, Luke's wife, Martha, packed up an' moved over to 'er sister's, until Luke had his course finished. She told how Luke 'ud get up in his sleep, go to the gramaphone, thinkin' it wuz his outdoor motor, hitch a piece o' string on the post in the center an' try to start 'er. She used to send over a box o' Nerve Food every week. Luke never took 'em but he give 'em to the young ingineer, Joe Manning. Joe claimed that wuz the only thing that saved 'im from goin' crazy while he wuz teachin' the old man.

"I remember the first day Luke come out fishin'. I wuz out on the ground, fishin' away, when all of a sudden I hears this queer hum. I couldn't make out first if it wuz an airplane or a 'hosstinger.' I looked all around, couldn't see nothin', but the hum got louder and louder. Then, up over a lop, I sees Luke's little crookeed-nose punt, goin' like the divil terryfied, an' Luke back on the countersate, grinin' all over his face. He cocked up his leg as he whipped along an' shouted out that he'd give me a tow if I wuz ready to go in when he wuz.

"Everything seemed to be comin' his way fer a while. He painted a name on the bow of his punt. Called 'er the *Hummin' Bird*, and hum she sartinly did. When Luke 'ud get in, just afore dark, all the young gaffers 'ud be down on the wharves, watchin' the *Hummin' Bird* dock, and all this attention made the old feller perk up still more. It got so bad that the rest of us wuz beginnin' to think about gettin' outdoors too, an' two or three of us had sent away for a catalog, when something happened which made us change our minds.

"One evenin' I got in afore Luke, an' a crowd of us was gettin' ready to go squiddin' when we heard the *Hummin' Bird* comin'. We didn't pay much attention till she got quite handy, and then somebody shouts, 'He can't stop 'er! Something's wrong with Luke's outdoor motor!' That made us look pretty fast. Sure enough, he couldn-t get 'er shot off, so he had to turn 'er out to sea agin, or she'd uv stove 'er stem in agin the peer.

"Well, holy ole mackerel, then the fun sturted. Four times he hove around an' made fer the wharf, an' four times he had to sheer off. Luke wuz frantic. The outdoor wuz putterin' away as if he wuz two miles out to sea instid of 'longside his own stage-head. Everybody sturted shoutin' advice, but by this time Luke wuz too far gone to take it, even if it had been any good. 'Don't the *Hummin Bird* know 'er nest when she gets to it?' bawled Bert Simmonds. 'What's the matter, Luke?' somebody else shouted. 'Did ya just remember the old woman promised ya a lickin' the minit ya stepped ashore?'

"By this time people had come from all around the cove and the fuss wuz tee-rific. An' then Luke got out his oars an' tried to stop 'er. But 'twas useless. He could only row about one horse power and the motor wuz four. We wuz all doin' our best to encourage 'im, goin' with our arms like we wuz rowin'. Aunt Sarah Coles, Luke's sister, rowed so hard, she fell over backwards, sprained 'er ankle, an' a couple o' men had to carry 'er 'ome on a handbar.

"All this time Luke's wife wuz tryin' ti find Joe Manning, so he could tell Luke wot to do. Well, sir, the last we saw of Luke fer a while, the oars had caught agin his chest, on account of the punt goin' so fast round an' round, an' knocked him down in the bottom of 'er outa sight. He wuz headin' straight out to sea then, an' the outdoor wuz goin' as strong as ever. He had filled 'er up with gas when he left the fishin' grounds. A full hour he had to keep cruisin' round the cove till she run outa oil, an' then he landed. The next day he sold 'er to Joe Manning fer half wot he paid."

Arthur Scammell

14

Arthur Scammell was born on Change Islands, Notre Dame Bay, in 1913. At the age of 15 he wrote "The Squid-jigging Ground", which launched a literary career spanning half a century. As a teacher he worked in various outports, but spent the greater part of his career in Montreal. He is represented in several anthologies, and frequently writes for periodicals. After retirement from high school teaching he served on the staff of Memorial University's English Department for several years. He lives in St. John's with his wife Rella.

Questions

1. What is the purpose of this essay and how does the illustration which is given develop the purpose?

2. Why is Scammell's style of writing particularly suitable for his subject?

3. The humour in this writing comes from character and situation. Comment on why this is so humourous to us.

Activities

1. Present this selection as a dramatic monologue by Skipper Neddie.

2. Using standard English try to make clear descriptions for the following words as they are used in this passage:

   punt   lop
   countersate   gaffers
   hosstinger   handbar
   outdoor motor

3. Use *The Dictionary of Newfoundland English* to assist you. Remember a senior citizen friend may be able to help by sketching a handbar or a punt.

4 Scammell's writings are best when read aloud. Another such writer was Ted Russell. Listen to *Tales from Pigeon Inlet* and *The Chronicles of Uncle Mose* — two very enjoyable recordings from Pigeon Inlet Productions.

Ray Guy's concentration on sensations in the following selection shows how writing about the familiar or commonplace need never be trite or banal. Fresh and unusual word choice transforms even the most routine activity such as eating into an interesting and, in this case, humourous event. The use of onomatopoeia, alliteration and vivid adjectives clarifies the descriptions and arouses the senses. A variety of sentence lengths along with original comparisons interspersed with a philosophic logic make this selection, on the one hand, light-hearted; on the other, revealing.

What A Charm, What A Racket

Let us turn now to the quiet nostalgia of simpler times, and read from *Guy's Encyclopedia of Juvenile Outharbour Delights.* We open to the entry on "Stimulating the Outharbour Juvenile's Senses."

This has to do with the various sensations open to the outharbour juvenile. Or, rather, which used to be open to him.

There used to be loud bangs in the night then. Well, less like a bang and more like a loud "pong." I always thought, until recently, that they were caused by the bigger boys out late on the roads firing rocks down at the fishermen's empty Acto casks on the stagehead.

But these later years I found out that the heat from the sun used to make the barrels puff up in the daytime and in the night when they cooled off they'd make a loud "pong."

You could hear all this going on from up in the bunk. You could hear all sorts of transactions. I always had the fashion of sleeping with my head as handy to the window as possible.

Calm nights when it was foggy and the window was up a bit and there was hardly enough breeze to knock the curtain scrim about, you could hear the long, slow grind of the tide on the beaches very far away.

You could hear a tin can bonking against the strouters or the rocks down there in the landwash, and you could hear the scattered peep of a cocksparrow almost too groggy to keep his eyes open.

First thing you could hear in the mornings was a few woody sort of klunks and the punt oars where the fishermen were shoving off to their collars.

Then you would hear the splashings where they were bailing her out with the piggin if it had rained the night before, and then you would hear a few "pffttttts" from the priming cup, a few backfires and then "chunck-chunck-chunck" right out through the harbour.

Some people say it is "buck-buck-buck-buck" but I think that would be more like your Atlantic than your average Acadia.

At that hour in the morning you didn't hear them talking to each other very much. Finally, when the whole chorus of motorboats had started up and faded away out the harbour, you would hear a rooster crowing somewhere over across the mesh.

Houses in those days, although a bit airish, were wonderfully suited to hearing what was going on outof doors.

It might be worth anyone's while even in this day and age to have one bedchamber that is not stuffed and stogged up with insulation and double pane glass.

You could hear every pat of the rain on the roof, every howl and whistle and squeak when it blew, you knew exactly what transactions were going on out doors without getting out of bed.

Apart from that, the frost which forms on the single-glass windowpane is quite interesting to the juvenile. All the trees and ferns and stuff. When they're frosted right up you can either blow a hole in them with your breath to see out, or you can lodge your tongue on them — if you want it peeled. Or you can make the print of your hand.

When the juvenile was laid up in bed with the measles and so forth he could hear a slow "chuff, chuff, chuff" noise in his head and a distant ringing like somebody frying in a frying pan.

On windy nights there was always a bottle howling somewhere — that is to say, the wind blowing across the neck of the bottle. Never failed. Always the neck of an empty bottle cocked up to the wind whichever way it blew.

Even when all the rest of the racket stopped you could always hear a peculiar and very small "click, click, click" from somewhere down around the baseboards. Some people called it the deathwatch.

Say about the middle of February when the lambs came along, the sheep used to kick up the hell of a racket in the evenings, sunny evenings, when people brought them up some scraps and hauled down a bit of hay to them.

This Russian person, Chagall, paints pictures of sheep just the spitting image of those ones, as I have discovered in my later years.

In the winter, in the woods, coming down the slide paths you would hear the bells jingling on the horses to give anyone coming along the path against them a chance to find a good place to haul off to one side.

Or you could hear the screech of the slide runners when they hit a patch of gravel and, if it was dark enough, see the sparks fly off.

Horses tackled up in the summer used not to be all the time bolting about like the ones we see in the western motion pictures. You could hardly hear them put their hocks down for the scrunching of the box cart wheels or the long cart wheels on the gravel.

One funny thing about sounds had to do with the school bell. In September it started off so merry. But by the time June came it sounded like the most dreariest thing in the world. We used to think that the clapper in it was getting sick and tired of being beat around.

The best time the church bell sounded was when it came from a long distance and you got a glimpse of it when the wind baffled.

When there was a funeral they would toll it slow and it was just like one hell of a big water tap with a very slow drip of holy water. Even when there was a gale of wind the church bell tolling for a funeral made it sound dead calm.

If you were going to have weather it was no trouble to hear the railway train blowing and that three mile away. When you were really going to have weather you could even hear the engines.

Nearly every outharbour mother has got the lungs of one of them opera singers. They could split your ears if you happened to be standing alongside of them and they were singing out to their own youngsters to come down and go up to the shop for them.

In the evenings they all got going at the one time singing out to their youngsters wherever they were to come in and get their suppers. Talk about making the valley ring! No need for loud speakers in those days.

Hearing people sawing off wood was as common as dirt, of course, up on what they called their "chipyard" and you could also hear them cleaving it up and the axe strike and then rending the junks apart with their hands and chucking it into the pile.

Hens were comical in the mornings when you went up to look in the hen's house. They'd be all hunched down on the nest looking sour as the cats, trying to get their eggs along and sputtering and grumbling to themselves.

What they said was, "Quarrk, quarrk. Puck-puck-puck, puck — AARRFFFF!" But us wicked little boys, though laced to Sunday School regular, used to say that what they were saying was something else! These days that is nothing at all.

You would hear the weather birds in the spring in the evenings when you were up playing rounders, and what birds they seemed to be who could fly so high no one could see them but make so loud a noise that everyone could hear them.

I didn't like it at all when someone told me that it was only the bloody snipes diving down through the air and making the noise with their wings. What is the need of telling people old stuff like that?

I saw it explained the other day why there was a sound when there was no sound at all. A person was giving a talk on radio and said that some people's ears when they are only youngsters can even hear the molecules of air striking against their eardrums.

Certainly, lots of other people must have had that experience too. It is an odd sound. It is not the same as when you are laid up in bed with the chicken pox, but sounds much more good like it is the sound the whole world is making.

But sounds were only a part of the sensations assailing the young Outharbor Juvenile's senses. What feeds they used to have! Not way back in the pod auger days, mind you. That was before my time. I mean not long ago, just before the tinned stuff and the packages and the baker's bread started to trickle into the outports.

Out where I come from the trickle started when I was or seven years old. One day I went next door to Aunt Winnie's (that's Uncle John's Aunt Winnie) and she had a package of puffed rice someone sent down from Canada.

She gave us youngsters a small handful each. We spent a long time admiring this new exotic stuff and remarking on how much it looked like emmets' eggs. We ate it one grain at a time as if it were candy, and because of the novelty didn't notice the remarkable lack of taste.

"Now here's a five cent piece and don't spend it all on sweets mind." You never got a nickel without this caution attached.

Peppermint knobs. White capsules ringed around with flannelette pink stripes. Strong! You'd think you were breathing icewater. They're not near as strong today.

Chocolate mice shaped like a crouching rat, chocolate on the outside and tough pink sponge inside. Goodbye teeth. Bullseyes made from molasses. And union squares — pastel blocks of marshmallow.

Those mysterious black balls that were harder than forged steel, had about 2,537 different layers of colour and a funny tasting seed at the centre of the mini-universe.

Soft drinks came packed in barrels of straw in bottles of different sizes and shapes and no labels. Birch beer, root beer, chocolate, lemonade, and orange.

Spruce beer, which I could never stomach, but the twigs boiling on the stove smelled good. Home brew made from "Blue Ribbon" malt and which always exploded like hand grenades in the bottles behind the stove.

Rum puncheons. Empty barrels purchased from the liquor control in St. John's. You poured in a few gallons of water, rolled the barrel around, and the result was a stronger product than you put down $15.00 a bottle for today.

Ice cream made in a hand-cranked freezer, the milk and sugar and vanilla in the can in the middle surrounded by ice and coarse salt. I won't say it was better than the store-bought stuff today but it tasted different and I like the difference.

Rounders (dried tom cods) for Sunday breakfast without fail. Cods heads, boiled sometimes, but mostly stewed with onions and bits of salt pork.

Fried cod tongues with pork scruncheons. Outport soul food. Salt codfish, fish cakes, boiled codfish and drawn butter, baked cod with savoury stuffing, stewed cod, fried cod.

Lobsters. We always got the bodies and the thumbs from the canning factories. When eating lobster bodies you must be careful to stay away from the "old woman," a lump of bitter black stuff up near the head which is said to be poisonous.

I was always partial to that bit of red stuff in lobster bodies but never went much on the pea green stuff although some did.

We ate turrs (impaled on a sharpened broomstick and held over the damper hole to singe off the fuzz), some people ate tickleaces and gulls but I never saw it done.

We ate "a meal of trouts," seal, rabbits that were skinned out like a sock, puffin' pig (a sort of porpoise that had black meat), mussels and cocks and hens, otherwise known as clams, that squirt at you through air holes in the mud flats.

Potatoes and turnips were the most commonly grown vegetables although there was some cabbage and carrot. The potatoes were kept in cellars made of mounds of earth lined with sawdust or goosegrass. With the hay growing on them they looked like hairy green igloos.

A lot was got from a cow. Milk, certainly, and cream and butter made into pats and stamped with a wooden print of a cow or a clover leaf, and buttermilk, cream cheese. And I seem to remember a sort of jellied sour milk. I forget the name but perhaps the stuff was equivalent to yogurt.

There was no fresh meat in summer because it wouldn't keep. If you asked for a piece of meat at the store you got salt beef. If you wanted fresh beef you had to ask for "fresh meat."

Biscuits came packed in three-foot long wooden boxes and were weighed out by the pound in paper bags. Sultanas, dad's cookies, jam jams, lemon creams with caraway seeds, and soda biscuits.

Molasses was a big thing. It was used to sweeten tea, in gingerbread, on rolled oats porridge, with sulphur in the spring to clean the blood, in bread, in baked beans, in 'lassie bread.

It came in barrels and when the molasses was gone, there was a layer of molasses sugar at the bottom.

Glasses of lemon crystals or strawberry syrup or lime juice. Rolled oats, farina, Indian meal. Home-made bread, pork buns, figgy duff, partridgeberry tarts, blanc mange, ginger wine, damper cakes.

Cold mutton, salt beef, peas pudding, boiled cabbage, tinned bully beef for lunch on Sunday, tinned peaches, brown eggs, corned caplin. And on and on the list inexhaustible and the young juvenile never reluctant to sample the provender provided.

But tastes these days seem not to have the same pungence and distinction. There is a great sameness about them all. Even the salt seems to have lost its savour. Smells, though, are still in fashion.

Some people are greatly taken with smells. The advertisers have got them frightened to death. They think they're a walking mass of rot and corruption from toes to crown, mobile compost heaps; and have to wage a daily battle to overcome the odour with all kinds of perfume.

They not only douse themselves with it but some of them must stew in tubsful overnight. There are men going about smelling like Christmas cakes baking in the oven. And women like lilac bushes after a thunder squall. You can see the fumes rising like heat off the pavement.

It is overdone. People don't stink more now than they always did. And even if they did nobody would notice except small children. They're the only ones who can still smell. The rest of us have got our smelling apparatus burnt out with cigarette smoke, car fumes and all the other dirt that's floating around in the air.

Take myself. I have been blessed by Nature with a splendid — some would say noble — piece of olfactory gear. I don't mean to boast, but it is one of my better features. Generous in proportion, robust if not elegant in outline, and topped off by two substantial holes at the bottom. You would think, then, that I could pick up a sour grape at fifty paces. No, sir. All this magnificent equipment has fallen into scandalous disrepair through lack of exercise and through the criminal, filthy and silly habit of cigarette smoking. That, plus the bit of pollution in the St. John's air.

It has been recommended by the municipal beautification committee that I take up some form of exercise to get in better physical shape and thus combat urban blight. I believe I'll exercise my beak. It's not too strenuous and about my speed. I'm reading the book: "Ten Easy Steps to a More Powerful Proboscis."

By such means we may all regain something of that nasal talent with which we were born. Ah, and what a myriad of delightful scents and odours crossed the keen hawse-holes of the Outharbour Juvenile as he commenced to plough the ocean of life!

Christmas cakes and lilac bushes aren't the only pretty scents. There are certain combinations of smells and sounds that the Outharbour Juvenile in particular associates with something in his earliest youth.

A bell in a steeple will give him a mental whiff of that bottle of scent known as "Evening in Church." It was the ruddy boredom which makes the churchy smell linger in memory.

Smelling was about the only diversion left open to him. He could get away for only a minute or two with fluttering the palms of his hands against his ears to make the hymns sound like acid rock music. An unobtrusive but telling clout to the short ribs cut that off in a hurry.

He couldn't look around to see how people were putting their mouths in all shapes singing while the rest of their faces remained deadly serious. He could only sit there and smell.

Dust and dilapidated cobwebs. Sun-warmed varnish. Mothballs off people's Sunday suits. Musty prayer books. Puffs of sharp coal smoke from the backfiring stoves. Aluminum paint or "Black Dazzle" on the stove pipes burning. A sniff of chilled blood from the coppers for the plate. Liniment and Friars Balsam and oil of wintergreen with which the old folk anointed themselves continually. That's what the sound of a church bell smells like.

Back when we had good nose-sight there was a full menu. Paint in the house in the spring — linseed oil and turpentine, not the new muck which smells like rancid blanc mange. People's wool clothes scorching against the stove in winter. New floor canvas and blasty boughs burning.

The best ones were in the fish store. Lovely, altogether lovely. Dried fish in heaps, tarred lines and hemp rope and barked nets and wood shavings under the bench and the sun on the felt on the roof. That is what the better land smells like.

"Better land" we say, but is that what we mean? For there is not much of the smell of land in Newfoundland. Only a bit from the bakeapple bogs at the end of July and the steam flying out of the potato ground on the first warm days in June.

When you think you smell nothing here what you are smelling is the salt water. It is in all the air so much that it goes unnoticed. When you go upalong in the summer and step off the plane at, say, Toronto, you will see the difference.

Then you are in the midst of a vast ocean of land. The only thing you can smell is earth. Not swampy, but steamy and warm with not a hint of cool in it. You may have to fight off slight panic at first because it feels like you are smothering in a sea of warm mud.

We see that an American company has put out a phonograph record which consists entirely of the sound of the sea rolling in on a beach.

It is selling well. People who live in big cities play it to drown out the sound of jet planes taking off and of people injuring each other in the streets outside. Perhaps we can put the smell of salt water into spray cans and sell it to them to go with their records.

Anyway, we could all get better mileage than we do out of our schnozolas. One of these days I'm going to try once again to leave off this ruddy nonsense of smoking cigarettes, because this Country is more delicious to look at than ever, and anyone who can't get a good whiff of her is not getting his just deserts.

Ray Guy

Ray Guy, a native of Arnold's Cove, Newfoundland, and winner of the Stephen Leacock Award for *That Far Greater Bay*, has published recently *Beneficial Vapours* and *An Heroine for Our Time*. He writes regularly for *Atlantic Insight* and *The Newfoundland Quarterly*. His humour covers a wide variety of types from satire to whimsey. Beneath many of his words describing our own province in earlier years we sense an appreciation for the "quiet nostalgia of simpler times."

Questions

1. What is nostalgia? What brings on Ray Guy's nostalgia?

2. How is the conversational style of this selection developed?

3. What writing techniques can you identify in Mr. Guy's style? Which seem to be used most effectively?

4. Choose your favourites from the listings of smells, sounds and foods. Can you explain your choice(s)?

Activities

1. Arrange a time and prepare some traditional Newfoundland recipes. Invite two or three guests who are not from our province. (A class dinner, perhaps).

2. Think about six of your own favourite sounds. Put these on tape and share with classmates to see similarities.

3. List smells you associate with pleasant memories — with unpleasant memories. Compare with someone else.

4. Expose your senses to pollution-free air. Take a hike to an untouched area near your school or home — a pond, the ocean, the woods.

5. "Clear, crisp and delightful — one of those perfect days when the atmosphere is so pure and transparent that minute objects can be distinguished for miles" says Wallace in *Lure of the Labrador Wild*. Read the book and note the many, many appeals to the senses.

6. A poem in which excellent examples of onomatopoeia are found is "The Kallyope Yell" by Vachel Lindsay in *Theme and Image*. Please read.

Often non-fiction is regarded by students as dull stuff. "The Wreck of the Florizel" goes a long way toward dispelling such an idea. Reading this selection, we are placed right on board ship alongside Third Officer Jackman on that fateful night of February 23, 1918. The atmosphere created in Brown's writing subtly draws the reader into the total experience. Dread rises and when disaster strikes we are not surprised; we felt it coming. Man and his ship are no match for the mighty hand of nature.

"The Wreck of the *Florizel*" (Excerpts)

Fate, the weaver, selected with infinite patience and delicacy a thread here, a thread there, uniting the various strands of life into a pattern of disaster. One hundred and thirty-eight souls would be tried and tested by the terrible destiny that awaited them. Others would be discarded before the design was complete — only later would they know that Fate spared them.

* * *

The victim chosen for this experience was the S.S. *Florizel*, of the prestigious Bowring's Red Cross Line, a large sturdy ship of 3,081 tons gross weight, 305 feet in length with a 42-foot beam. She had four decks, four holds, and accommodations for 145 first-class and 36 second-class passengers. She was splendidly furnished, richly carpeted, upholstered in plush, finished in oak and mahogany and costly green tapestry.

* * *

Because of the war she had not gone to the seal hunt since 1915, but she had crossed the Atlantic several times with volunteers for the slaughter that was taking place in Europe. The *Florizel*'s main function, however, was the St. John's-Halifax-New York run, with the odd Caribbean cruise thrown in. The agents who booked passengers and cargo were Harvey and Company, Ltd., a large and prestigious firm.

* * *

At 7:30 p.m. on February 23, 1918, the order "Full Astern!" was piped down to the engine room. Blowing her whistle, the *Florizel* backed away from the wharf into midstream, a dark, hulking shadow, with all portholes, windows, and skylights covered and only her navigation lights showing against the great bulk of the Southside Hills that formed a rampart against the Atlantic. She was soon steaming out through The Narrows, her automatic whistle sounding frequently, warning all to make way.

Thus the *Florizel* began her last voyage, into the pages of history.

Because of the wind direction, the sonorous tones of her whistle hung over the town, each blast sounding for eight seconds exactly. The townspeople paused in their activities and gave her their full attention, listening intently as the blasts gradually faded, straining to catch the last lonely sound. Many would later recall that a strange, unsettled feeling came over them after she had gone.

* * *

For the passengers, the excitement of leaving port gradually waned, and they gathered in the social hall or the smoker.

* * *

The bar had opened and the party atmosphere continued; the slow rolling of the ship, the staggering hesitant movements of the passengers added to the general merriment. Full of confidence and good spirits, the young men grouped noisily together; there was good-natured ribaldry and bursts of laughter as they compared good times. Presently one of them sat at the piano and began to play, "It's a Long Way to Tipperary." Immediately, others drifted to the piano and the lusty sound of voices rang through the hall....

* * *

The *Florizel* passed Cape Spear and kept on steaming until the Cape bore west by south, an estimated one and a half to two miles at 8:30 p.m. Taking a bearing by Cape Spear light, Captain Martin altered course to southwest, then ten minutes later altered to southwest-quarter-south, allowing a quarter point to make a good southwest course to offset the possibility of an indraft setting in on the Cape, which might nudge her shoreward. Once around Cape Spear, she had the powerful Polar Current that swept along Newfoundland's northeast coast. The official speed of the Polar Current was from one to one and a half knots and was always of assistance to ships steaming southward to Cape Race, although with a northeast wind Captain Martin found it had a speed of from one and a half to two knots.

Most Newfoundland mariners believed in "giving danger a wide berth" and sailed out into the Atlantic beyond Cape Spear for several miles before turning southward when bad weather signs were so evident. Captain Martin ignored the warning signals and steamed along the shore on his regular fine-weather course, less than two miles offshore.

To the starboard, through the thickening haze, Captain Martin could see the dark bulk of Motion Head, a distance of six to seven miles along the coast. The wind was freshening; it had backed from the southwest to the south-southwest since they had left port, and was hitting the *Florizel* about a point on the starboard bow. A swell was running dead on her bow, causing the ship to plunge a little. The swells were not heavy, and the sish ice kept them from breaking. Although the wind and the sea were against her, Captain Martin was confident that the Polar Current would offset any hindrance from that direction. By one o'clock she would be round Cape Race and well on her way to Halifax.

* * *

The weather continued to deteriorate. The haze had thickened

26

perceptibly, obscuring the land. The coastline from Cape Spear to Cape Race was precipitous and dangerous, looming over the sea and making it a very dark stretch of coast. Tonight it was blacker than usual.

deteriorate. The haze had thickened perceptibly, obscuring the land. The coastline from Cape Spear to Cape Race was precipitous and dangerous, looming over the sea and making it a very dark stretch of coast. Tonight it was blacker than usual.

On the bridge, Third Officer Jackman became more alert, looking for landmarks that would show him the progress they were making, but he could distinguish nothing: the coast was a murky bulk, slightly blacker than the blackness of the night. With no log streaming, there was no way he could know for sure at what speed they were travelling. He did know the ship was still lagging.

He paced the bridge uneasily, eyes raking the night. The wind was rising and backing to the southward and was blowing dead on her bow; the ice, propelled by the wind and sea, was pressing against her. It was a combination he did not like, particularly along this shore. Suddenly he felt uncomfortable; his nostrils twitched; he had the distinct impression that the land to the west was looming closer.

Was the *Florizel* sagging into Petty Harbour Bay?

Were they off course?.

* * *

Captain Martin assessed the situation. If the *Florizel* had sagged in on the land and there was no light to guide them, it was imperative that they try to establish how close she was to land. Ordinarily the sounding lead would indicate their position, but soundings along the southern shore, from Cape Spear to the south of Ferryland (roughly 30 miles), hardly varied at all on the normal course of the ship and, because of it, the lead was considered practically useless in thick weather. However, soundings would show if she was *inside* her course. He passed the order to Jackman: "Get the sounding lead."

The sounding apparatus consisted of a wire on a reel with lead weighing 28 pounds. The lead had a hollow bottom filled with soap, tallow, or grease, so that when it hit bottom, whatever was on the ocean floor adhered to it and gave mariners an idea what they were travelling over; it helped identify their position.

Connected to the line was a brass tube into which a chemically coated glass tube had to be inserted. When the apparatus plunged to the sea bed, the pressure of the water forced the chemical up inside the glass tube and indicated the depth of water they were steaming over. The *Florizel* carried about 60 sounding tubes.

Martin himself inserted a glass sounding tube in the brass tube. The apparatus was then passed to Seaman Dooley and Seaman Gover, who carried it aft where the sounding gear was located. It was 10:10 p.m.

Martin and Jackman, hypersensitive to the dropping of the atmospheric pressure, paced the bridge restlessly, stopping in the wings to stare at the ice along her side. They decided that it was not packing; in fact, it appeared to be very loose.

* * *

The *Florizel* now began to pitch and roll in the cross-sea sending most of her passengers reeling to their cabins.

* * *

Philip Jackman, staring down at the heaving seas, could not delude himself that the *Florizel*'s speed had increased. Beside him, Captain Martin's stocky figure was hunched over the starboard railing, eyes riveted to the ice.

Both men were more puzzled than ever. With the telegraph set at "Full Speed" it could not be assumed she was doing less.

* * *

The heavy swells were beginning to "heave home" now with the force of the Atlantic behind them, and even with the sish ice to quiet them, they fell in tumbled confusion on top of each other. Labouring, the *Florizel* steamed on a south-southwest course that would take her away from the dangerous coast.

* * *

The *Florizel*'s movements grew more lively as the sea and wind shifted around to the southeast. Labouring through the heavy cross-sea, she jumped and reeled as the swells careered in different directions.

* * *

The wind steadily freshened, singing around the bridge, rattling the lifeboats in the davits. When it gusted, the snow swept across the deck in blinding sheets, piling up in every corner and crevice. By 2:00 a.m. the wind had backed right out to the southeast on the *Florizel*'s beam, and the sea had followed, so that the cross-sea gradually merged with the swells, which rolled dead on her port beam with the awesome force of a thousand miles of ocean behind them. Now she began to steam through small patches of open sea. The phosphorescent glitter of cresting waves loomed here and there, a savage flicker of white.

* * *

Captain Martin had returned to the bridge, pacing with Second Officer King. The barometer was still falling and the black night pressed around them. Puzzled as he was about the ship's lack of speed, Martin still did not question the engine room crew. He was confident that she was safely off the land; the sou'sou'west course since midnight had taken the *Florizel* well outside the shallow waters of the Bantems, and except for the swell and the wind on her beam, which appeared to be slowing her, all was well. He was absolutely sure she was out into the deep Atlantic, so sure that he had not bothered to take any soundings after midnight.

* * *

By 3:30 a.m. they had steamed into clear water, and the sea, released from the confines of ice, crested and showed its teeth; swells with ugly white tops reared on the *Florizel*'s beam, pitched her madly to starboard. In the staterooms, luggage began to slide and roll about the floors, wardroom doors crashed open and clothes danced wildly on hangers like puppet scarecrows. Passengers clutched the wooden sideboards of their berths to keep from being flung to the floor; a few were still wretchedly ill.

* * *

On the bridge, Captain Martin peered through the black night. He was confident that as soon as they rounded Cape Race and ran under the lee of the land, the sea would lose much of its fury. They were, he estimated, in the process of rounding the Cape, and passengers would shortly be able to rest easier; the cargo would be secured.

Beside him, First Officer James peered through the night and thought he saw something solid white ahead.

Ice!

Was that more ice glimmering on the black sea?

A sleety rain still raked the ship, but he could see up to three-quarters of a mile, he estimated.

Was that ice ahead?

His eyes narrowed. It looked like one of the strings they had been passing through earlier; he could see the dark sea beyond.

Captain Martin saw it at the same time. "What's that?" he snapped. "It looks like ice."

"Yes, it does," James agreed, but to be sure he examined the white line through the binoculars as they pitched and rolled toward it. He said slowly, "Yes, I believe it is."

Martin also scrutinized it through the binoculars as the *Florizel* hurtled onward. It was ice, he decided. "Probably a string of slob coming around the Cape."

* * *

The *Florizel*, steaming a good nine to ten knots, with the wind and sea snarling on her port quarter, bounded along toward the white line.

But the white line was not a string of ice, it was a white line of breakers 250 yards offshore from Horn Head Point, Cappahayden, 45 miles along the coast from Cape Spear, 12 miles north of Cape Race.

There was a grinding, screeching crash of metal on rock as the *Florizel* piled onto the reef. Riding high on the crest of a swell, she fell on the rocks, hitting under number-two hold, to be lifted by a following wave and carried farther over the rocks. A third time she was lifted and dropped in a welter of furious seas. Her foretopmast crashed to the foredeck, rocks gouged and tore her hull; then, securely impaled, she began to grind and settle to the starboard. Cradled on a slope with bow up and stern down the proud *Florizel* was mortally wounded, with a gaping hole in her starboard side and the bottom torn out of her.

Captain Martin had run her full speed upon Horn Head Reef.

* * *

Then, because she was an obstruction to its forward drive, the ocean gathered in upon itself and lifted over her port quarter to smash upon her deck. Great combers surged up over her port side, heaved over the bulwarks to explode against the superstructure with awesome force. Ladders and doors on the port side gave way and the sea rushed in through the social hall, cascaded down over the great ornate stairway, and fell through the circular opening above the dining saloon.

Skylights were shattered. The seas swept her diagonally on the promenade deck; the port doorway aft leading into the first-class section, and the starboard doorway leading to the officers' quarters below, shook ominously. The crash had shifted many of the wartime blackouts on the superstructure and, like a leviathan, she lay there, her lights blazing, her automatic whistle wailing as the heavy seas toyed with her.

* * *

Waves were piling in from the Atlantic, rearing to great heights and rolling shoreward in a seething, tumbling mass. They fell upon the *Florizel* with such violence as to preclude any attempt to rig lifelines. All such lines and safety equipment were swept away.

She shook continually, her metal plates clanking against the rocks. With the bottom torn out of her, the holds and the engine room filled quickly. The water, rushing through the narrow passageways on the lower deck, rose with deadly swiftness. Heavy swells billowed up over the port quarter to fall over on her deck and smash against the superstructure; they raked her diagonally, with the whole port side taking the brunt of the terrible force of the ocean.

Suddenly the port door aft burst inward, and the water tunneled in through the alleyway, boiling furiously as it smashed head on into the sea flowing back from the social hall. It rushed into the cross-alleyway at the foot of the smoker stairway, spilled over the stairs to the saloon deck. The same wave split the rear starboard door leading directly to the crew's quarters below. In a few minutes the cross-alleyway leading to the crew's quarters was a rushing torrent of water.

As the ocean invaded her, the wind carried her death cries in over the land.

Cassie Brown
(from *A Winter's Tale*)

Cassie Brown has become quite well know nationally and internationally for her non-fiction, particularly her books dealing with Newfoundland sea disasters. The fine attention to precise detail, the expert understanding of real people and the exact order of actual events draw readers to each of her books. She makes us feel the sense of fatalism which permeates her work.

Questions

1. How does the author personify fate? Do you like the personification?

2. What effect does atmosphere and setting have on the reader in this selection? What is the role of premonition?

3. Where does blame for this tragedy appear to belong? Explain.

4. Notice how time is treated. How does the author make one feel the realistic passage of time?

Activities

1. On a detailed map of the area trace the intended and actual routes of the *Florizel*. Consult *A Winter's Tale* for extra information. Read the book.

2. The Newfoundland coast has been littered with shipwrecks. Try to find out about wrecks which may have occurred in the coastal area nearest you.

3. When you visit a museum look for a "sounding lead".

*In 1914 a young American named Rockwell Kent came to live in
Brigus, Newfoundland. He acquired an old house and soon became
part of that bustling fishing and seafaring community. In this account
he lets us feel the whole range of emotions adrift among the people
as a bright promising spring turns quickly to darkest storm and double
tragedy. Kent was sensitive enough to realize that he was experiencing
an event few of his generation of Americans could conceive of. His
account is included in his book* North by East, *which tells of a voyage
from New York to Greenland by sailboat.*

Brigus, Newfoundland

I hold a letter in my hand and read it:

> Dearest: There's a blizzard raging here in New York and we are
> terrified to think of what you must be suffering in Newfoundland.
> These few feet of snowfall and the zero cold that make so much misery
> here must mean mountains of snow for you and more intense cold
> than we know anything about. Be careful of yourself. Dress warmly.
> — Be sure to put on the bed socks and the woolen cap I made for you
> to wear at night.

Ha! I sit in the sunny, sheltered warmth of the doorstep of the old
house I am rebuilding, and read these cautions — smilingly. The last of
February — and in one day spring. The low sun shines almost from six to
six. Daily it melts the snow and softens the brown earth. The brooks are
full; they fill the air with their murmuring. Sea birds are singing. On my
snug hillside facing south the spring has come!

Each day of March was like the first but maybe fairer. The sun dried
the earth and brought out the green shoots of the grass in the wet lands. I
left off my heavy hide boots and danced about light-shod. The house was
nearly built and it was pretty to behold. I put a fence about it and a gateway
arched over with the rib of a boat.

* * *

Men from up the harbor had come almost daily to visit me. Old men they
mostly were, for the youth of the whole country were gone to the ice fields.
They stood with me on the warm hillside and thought, perhaps, of their
own youth, and told me what a place it was for courting in the springtime.
"Wait 'til the byes come back from the ice; with them and the girls you'll
have company enough. — This is the first place for dandelions — do you
like them? Ah, 'tis a great sight they are, stretching everywhere right down
to the water." My house stood out of the town and looked somewhat back
upon it over the harbour. I could see the schooners still quiet at their
moorings where the bustle of preparation for the Labrador would soon
begin.

* * *

Sunday night the twenty-ninth of March I went with Robert Percy to the Church of England, the church of my childhood, whose rector had officially called on me the day before and claimed me. This church was cozier than the great old tabernacle of the Methodists but it was awfully dull. It may be that the return of the young men from the ice fields will bring life to these services. We went out from the little church into the profound night. It was cold and the sky brilliantly starred. Over our left shoulders hung the new moon just setting. I thought it wonderfully beautiful. "That's a bad moon," said Robert Percy. "We'll have weather, for you can hang a powder horn on it." Sure enough the slender crescent lay almost fair on its back. I couldn't believe in the ill omen and questioned him. "I never knew it to fail," he answered.

* * *

I wake at six. I stick my nose and eyes out of my blankets and peer over the bulge of the feather bed to enquire the quality of the day. Through the upper sash of the little window, close beneath the eaves, I see the land across the harbour. If it be fair I know it before my eyes can focus on the far away illumined hills and houses for my room will be flooded with reflected sunlight. Tuesday morning, the last day of March, I looked, at six o'clock, through the three small panes of the upper sash into dull, blank grayness. I could only after a moment distinguish faintly the hills. Between, there fell a curtain of snow. I rose and lighted my fire and brought in coal, wood and water against the coming storm. The air was damp and icy; a strong wind had risen and was blowing the fine snow in gusts about the yard. My house is under the hill; no normal wind from North or East or West can touch it but in broken blasts. But, as the wind rose today and swept fiercely over the hills behind, it sought out every sheltered nook and, where it could not blow directly, penetrated by refraction. I could hear it from within doors about the chimney top; at first it made the fire roar, but finally entered the flue and blew the soft-coal smoke in clouds about the room. For an hour I stood it and then, taking from the mantel shelf my toothbrush, my razor, this tablet upon which I'm now recording the event, and a volume called *Old Faiths in New Light* which the Methodist parson had advanced to my for my conversion, and stowing all the rest away from the reach of soot, I went up the harbour. Along the road I began to realize the gravity of the storm. The snow was already deep and drifting heavily. The wind at my back hurried me along recklessly, plunging me into drifts and becoming actually dangerous where the road hung on the cliff-side over the harbour fifty feet below.

* * *

I spent the greater part of that day up the harbour. My dinner I had with Robert Percy and his family and repaid a bare spoonful of it by chopping up spruce boughs for the cow's bed. I returned to my house for a while in the afternoon though they begged me not to. Already the storm had risen

33

to such height of fierceness that there was dread in everyone's demeanor and a desire to keep men indoors. It was a battle to reach the place; the wind took the breath from my nostrils and stung my face with driving snow. Look into it I could not, but glimpses I caught abroad, beyond the very track I strove to follow, were of whole banks of snow in mid-air carried by the gale. At the house I lit my stove but put it out again in haste for the kitchen had been blown full of smoke. I abandoned the house and returned up the harbour before the wind. This was better. I looked as I went for the brooks that had murmured so pleasantly in the spring days just passed. They lay smothered under six feet of drifted snow.

I stamped and swept my feet in the Percy's hall. The people cried out with relief as I entered. To them all storms are ocean storms and they are terrible. I had never realized till that moment in the room that storm spells always death for some of the family of the followers of the sea.

In sealing, fortunes have been made. Towns have been built and have flourished with the dollars that the wooden fleets of old brought from the ice fields. They have decayed since steel and steam ruined their invested capital and built up the fleet of the merchants of St. John's. Men no longer take ship in their own harbours, but follow their captains to the metropolis to serve under them or where they may. Of the sailing fleet of St. John's were the steamers *Florizel* and *Stephano* of the Red Cross Line, the *Belleaventure* and the *Bonaventure*, the *Eric* that had been with Peary to the north, and the *Terra Nova* of the heroic Captain Scott, Shackelton's *Southern Cross*, the *Neptune, Viking, Newfoundland* and others.

* * *

I have not been to the ice but I believe that all men's work the world over is alike in wearisomeness, for men are not braver nor stronger here than there. For pay they receive a small part of the value of their labour, for their risks nothing. So the dangers are never counted. The fields of ice that float each spring through the gulf of St. Lawrence and the Atlantic east of Newfoundland, are the hunting ground of seal killers. In early morning the crews are set upon the ice. They wander the day long in quest of seals — miles separate them from their ships. A man may break his leg in the rough going, he may fall into the sea in crossing an open space, the ice field splits and opens a gulf of water that bars return, or a snow storm rising shuts everything from view and leaves the man alone and lost. The deaths in eighty years of sealing have been many hundreds.

I stood in the kitchen and Robert Percy spoke, — "The *Southern Cross* passed Channel Monday." This struck the keynote of the tension in the household; there was a murmur of sorrow. I looked at each and felt at once the gravity of the tidings. "This morning she passed St. Pierre and Miquelon. It's a hard chance she's got in this." The gale was terrible; the frosted panes had darkened the room and shut the storm from view, but the wind howled dismally in the flue and the old house creaked in its timbers like an ancient ship. We all huddled about the stove, no thought but of the storm and of the *Southern Cross*. The grandmother was remarkable. She had accepted the ship as lost from the first tidings of her.

The nobility of her mien had always impressed me. She was Grecian now in the austerity of her prophecy and grief. At tea time a man entered with news from the cable office. It was merely that no word had been heard of the missing ship. "It will pretty well clean out this place," he said. The grandmother rose with a cry of pain and left the room.

That night I got up to go, but they would not hear of it. An old woman that I had never seen knew of my being there that afternoon. "Don't let that man go home," she said. I am a new friend but if I had gone that night the women would not have slept. Nor would they let me lie on the couch in the kitchen. I went to bed with Robert Percy and saw and admired his old rose colored, home-knit drawers. A lamp burned all night on the hall floor and cast its light equally into all our bedrooms. In the hall the old clock struck the hours and half hours as the ship's bell sounds them.

Wednesday morning the wind blew unabated, but from the Westward. The aspect of the day was the same as yesterday; we could only guess that above the gray and drifting clouds of snow there was a fair sky. I went to find my house. It was there, of course, but hardly to be seen from far. The drifts upon the way were beyond belief, and at the house so coated were the windows as to make it dark within, almost to the need of lamplight. And my brook! Even the sloping valley sides were gone, filled level with the land above. One day had plunged us into deepest winter. Without water I could not comfortably live, so again I returned to the harbour. As I came up the road toward Percy's house I saw a knot of men about the door. The horror of the news they told, my God! I shall never forget. Last night the entire crew of the steamer *Newfoundland*, one hundred and sixty men, had frozen to death on the ice.

We can know little of such a death. At the store later that morning a man told this story. In 1898 he had gone to the ice. They entered the harbour of St. John's exulting in the sure hope of first arrival. But there before them at the wharf stood the tall masts of a sealer; they were beaten. They came to anchor and set ashore the bos'n and a small crew. The speaker was among them. As they neared the wharf he saw it to be crowded with men and that some carried their arms or legs in bandages. From the ship there were being borne frozen corpses. The bodies were mostly naked, stripped at death to save their comrades. They were in all attitudes, crouching, doubled up and straight, wide-eyed as if living, and grimacing. They were being chopped from a pile of ice aft on the vessel's deck. Forty-eight had perished from this ship — the *Greenland*.

Wednesday night I slept again with Robert Percy. It blew a gale and the night was thick with snow. I would have returned to my house for I had tried the road. But people were unnerved by now. Thursday and Friday and Saturday passed. The weather was still severe.   I dug into the drift and found water. I was out of coal and dragged a sackful laboriously over the snow from the town. All day of every day the cable office up the harbour was crowded with people. The reports were posted as they came; children acting as messengers copied them and carried them back. Survivors there proved to be of the *Newfoundland* and the list of perished fell to half the original report. It was still appalling beyond belief. But still of the *Southern Cross* no news was heard. The St. John's papers published a list of her officers and crew; they numbered upwards of one hundred and seventy. One pointed out to me the homes of some of these. The dread of the loss of this steamer had passed almost to certainty and the mention of the house, the wife, the children, the hopes and ambitions of any of those on her became a tragedy. The drama written in the loss of a hundred men is a world story. It includes all; mother-love, the tale of courtship, of youth, of marriage — it touches the whole gamut of emotion in ten thousand lives. The pastor visited the wife and daughter of the master of the *Southern Cross*. The wife had cried to exhaustion and the girl lay in half delirium calling for her father. This household was demoralized and little food had one tasted the week. On Tuesday the house had been swept and made ready for the father's return. That was the day that others knew that it would never be. There was another house where little food had been tasted those many days for poverty. A mother lay sick in bed of the birth of a seven months' child, that she had borne unattended. She had many small children and no grown person with her. The loss of the *Southern Cross* would drive her insane for her mind was weak and wandered at child birth.

The news that came on Saturday night was of a three masted ship seen in Placentia Bay and thought to be the *Southern Cross*. The message came privately to the druggist who was told to hold it until confirmation. So it flew like wildfire through the town and to the stricken homes. Before an hour it was contradicted, for the sighted ship was not the *Southern Cross*. This news was brought to us at the Percy home. On the *Southern Cross* they had no near relation, but grief among these people is not alone for those they are connected with. The mother had gone at the first news to the Master's wife and child. She returned crestfallen. There had been many at the house and though the callers soon learned of the denial of the rumour they had left the poor wife clinging to her hope. As the evening wore on and no word came she began to fear again and wept, begging to be told the truth. How terrible false hopes can be! Another woman, we were told, clung in her extremity to her belief in the unseen spirit of the dead. She cried, "I can't believe it for I have seen no token!" Can there be truth in tokens? In 1872 the *Village Bell* was at the ice. One night the wife of a man aboard her awoke. She heard the tramp of men on the street from the shore. They bore on their shoulders her husband's chest. At her gate they put it down heavily. She sprang from bed, went to the door and opened it. The night was empty of men and of sound and no chest was there. That night her husband and seventeen others perished on the ice. Another woman whose man was lost returning from the Labrador longed for a token. She rose each night and taking his clothes from the chest went about the house calling to him. "Would you speak to your husband if he came that way in the night?" asked someone among us. "I'd be afeared to!" said Robert's young wife, tensely. They spoke again of the unhappy wife and daughter and asked the grandmother, who was of distant kin, if she would visit them on the morrow. "No," she answered, "I called today. I told the girl she had lost as fine a father as there ever lived, but 'twas the will of God."

It is Monday the sixth of April, and the sun shines at last with the balm of returning spring. I stood naked out of doors at sunrise and felt its warmth, while my ears were filled with the sound of dripping snow. In a few days the last traces of this second winter will have disappeared from the land; the grass will resume its growing, the ancient lilac bush its budding, and one may look forward to the promised dandelions of June. The town across the harbour will appear again as serene and beautiful as on the spring morning of a week ago. Through the seasons forever it will turn its weatherbeaten face stolidly seaward and show, save in the gradual decay of its might, nothing of the calamities that have struck its heart.

Rockwell Kent
(from *North by East*)

Rockwell Kent was an artist and author with a great love for the sea. His adventures and voyages took him over many of the great oceans, from Alaska to Cape Horn to Greenland. His stay in Newfoundland came to a rather unhappy end when during the First World War he was suspected of spying and was asked to leave the country. His published works include *Wilderness*, *Voyaging*, and *North by East* from which this selection is taken. His illustrations are to be found in editions of *Candide*, *The Canterbury Tales*, and *Moby Dick*. *North by East* was published by Random House, and more recently by Wesleyan University Press, Middleton, Connecticut, in 1978.

Questions

1. Consider the writing style used by Mr. Kent. How would you describe it?

2. What characteristics of the people seem to appeal most to the young American? How does this contrast with the outcome of his stay in this country?

3. What is your response to the author's emphasis on weather to open and close the selection?

Activities

1. Find pictures of some of the sealing vessels named in the account. *The Newfoundland Fish Boxes* by Dr. Harry Roberts is a good place to start. Books by Cassie Brown will show others.

2. Discuss with others the indications of philosophy and religions affecting people's lives in this selection.

3. Find references to the tragedies in Newfoundland folk songs.

"Newfoundland Disaster (1914)" presupposes that you have read <u>Death on the Ice</u> *by Cassie Brown. The poem presents the sealers as victims of a tyrannical system motivated only by the quest for seals. The death imagery leaves a powerful picture of a poignant event in our history.*

Newfoundland Disaster (1914)
(after Cassie Brown)

It is a story
of heaving, blood-slicked decks
banshee shrieks in riggings
sun hounds portentous
in the east
and nightmare's drift across
uncertain dawns;
a tale of distances
between colonial men
who knew their stations
all too well
and ships with whistles silent
in March gales

Quiet men
who'd turned their backs
on tribal tyranny
raised faces against a storm
challenged the howl of death
till each last
voice and breath
became the wind

Their eulogies
were etched
on the scarred bows of ships
questing a pitiless harvest
somewhere
west of the Front

Enos Watts

Enos Watts, a teacher who now lives with his family in Stephenville, shows uncanny insight into people's lives, especially the people of our own province, past and present. His poetry can be found in anthologies such as *East of Canada* and *31 Newfoundland Poets*. Watts' poems often present harsh images of the even harsher scenes of real life, as can be seen in "Newfoundland Disaster (1914)".

Questions

1. Cyril Poole in "The Soul of a Newfoundlander" gives an interesting hypothesis regarding the Newfoundlander's desire to hunt. Read it. Does Watts' poem support or refute Poole's ideas? Explain clearly.

2. What motivated sealers to take risks such as were taken in the 1914 disaster.

3. Notice the omens in stanza one. How is this similar to "The Wreck of the *Florizel?*

4. Explain
   'banshee'
   'portentous'
   'eulogies'

Why are these words or phrases especially fitting?

Activities

1. Using charcoal, sketch the scene presented in stanza one.

2. Make a collage of pictures dealing with sealing.

3. Do some research on today's seal hunt. Draw comparisons with the early days of the hunt.

4. Why is "Front" capitalized? You may have to do a bit of research to find out. A sealer would likely be able to tell you why.

5. Find pictures of the "Newfoundland" disaster. David Blackwood's work is very graphic.

6. A young Newfoundlander refers to banshees in a poem entitled "Heritage", which can be found in "The Newfoundland Quarterly", Summer and Fall, 1981. Volume LXXVII, No. 2 & 3. Read it. It is most appropriate for this unit.

7. Read some more poems by Enos Watts in *After the Locusts*.

This expository essay is scholarly and formal. It contains effective reference material should one be doing research in such areas as sociology or cultural studies. The use of allusions is particularly noteworthy as these help establish tone and lend weight to the author's point of view that "we are all children of the sea".

The Soul of a Newfoundlander

Newfoundlanders are a peculiar people, a fact noted by many native and foreign observers. Indeed a large number of writers, including Moses Harvey and Joseph Hatton, Julian Moreton, George Allan England, J.R. Smallwood and Farley Mowat, have gone so far as to refer to us as a race. None of these writers, of course, used the term 'race' in its scientific sense. But it is revealing that they thought it natural to use the strongest term expressive of distinctness. It is stronger than 'tribe' or 'people.' That we are so distinct as to make the use of 'race' natural and easy is an observation also supported by Newfoundlanders abroad, who see us both from within and from outside. I take it for a fact, then, that we are a singular people or as our saying goes 'queer sticks.'

And we are all queer sticks, all bent the same way; for despite differences of origin, dialect and religion we are all children of the sea. That is what Pratt conveyed in "Erosion."

> It took the sea an hour one night,
> An hour of storm to place
> The sculpture of these granite seams
> Upon a woman's face.

No more imaginative title will ever be found for a study of the Newfoundland soul than Mowat's *This Rock Within the Sea*. Regarding the sea as our "ultimate existence", Mowat views us as "eminently successful survivors of an evolutionary winnowing process that few modern races have undergone."[1] That winnowing process was fishing from the great waters. As Al Pittman so aptly put it, the sea was "at once their sustenance and deprivation, their life and their death." [2]

A full explanation of our peculiarity would have to take several factors into account. Like all peoples we are partly children of our ancestors and of their history. Most of our traits are traceable to England's West Country and to Ireland. But there can be no doubt that they have been molded and magnified by our life on this island and in particular by the way we have earned our daily bread. In the lines of R.A. Parsons' major poem "Salute to Port de Grave", "for labours tend/To mark the labourers...."[3]

One of the striking traits of Newfoundlanders is our sense of fatalism. It has seeped into the very marrow of our bones. It found expression in our newspapers and literature, in a thousand sermons, and more significantly, in the very language of our people. There is, of course, a strain of fatalism in many peoples and certainly in some of our ancestors. But in Newfoundland it is so pronounced that in explaining it we must look for a peculiar cause. That factor is, I believe, centuries of dependence on the stormy North Atlantic. In his characterization of North Atlantic fishermen in *Grey Seas Under*, Farley Mowat caught the essence of this fatalism.

> They believe that man must not attempt to overmaster the primordial and elemental forces and break them to his hand. They believe that he who would survive must learn to be a part of the wind and water, rock and soil, nor ever stand in braggarts' opposition to these things. *(p.21)*

Contrasts between the tiller of the soil and the fisherman on the troubled waters of the North Atlantic shed much light on the Newfoundlander's fatalism. The contrast has been drawn by several observers. The writer who probed into our relation with the sea as brilliantly as it has ever been done was Norman Duncan. Born in Ontario in 1871, Duncan made several visits to Newfoundland and Labrador between 1900 and 1906. His keen observations of the fisherman's life and philosophy were published in several works, including *The Way of the Sea* (1903); *Dr. Luke of Labrador* (1904) and *Dr. Grenfell's Parish* (1905). The brilliance of Duncan's insights into the sea-touched character of the Newfoundlander has not been surpassed; not by George Allan England's *Vikings of the Ice* (republished in 1969 under the title *The Greatest Hunt in the World*), or even by Pratt's magnificent "Rachel." Duncan was particularly perceptive on the contrast between the farmer and the fisherman. Those who settle as farmers even in the remotest wilderness do so with the hope of taming it. As Duncan noted in *The Way of the Sea:*

> Now the wilderness, savage and remote, yields to the strength of men. A generation strips it...a generation tames it and tills it, a generation passes into the evening shadows as into rest in a garden, and thereafter the children of that place possess it in peace and plenty, through succeeding generations, without end, and shall to the end of the world. *(p.309).*

To till the soil is to enclose it against the beasts of the forest; to spread lime where there is acid; to fertilize when it is deficient; to irrigate against a drought and to ditch against the flood. In a word to till is to thwart laws of nature or at least to bend them to one's will.

But the fisherman can do none of these things. It is not given to him to still the waters. In language imitative of the rhythmic pounding of the seas on our rugged shores Duncan captured the contrast between land and sea:

> But the sea is tameless: as it was in the beginning, it is now and shall be — mighty, savage, dread, infinitely treacherous. ...yielding only that which is wrested from it, snarling, raging, snatching lives, spoiling souls of their graces....The deep is not...subdued; the toiler of the sea...is born to conflict, ceaseless and deadly and, in the dawn of all the days, he puts forth anew to wage it.[4]

As Duncan observed of an old Black Harbour skipper, "He did not know that in other lands the earth yields generously to the men who sow the seed." When the young boy Jack is told that some men in other places have never even seen the sea, he asks: "Sure, not a hundred haven't?" Told "More than that," he mutters, " 'tis hard t' believe, zur, terrible hard."[5]

That we who have for so long faced the sea bear its marks upon our countenance is a fact noted by other writers. As in "Rachel" and "Florizel", Pratt understood the powers of the sea, "a stark and wild inebriate", to sculpture granite seams in a face set against it. Writing in 1937, J.R. Smallwood also drew imaginative conclusions from the fact of our struggle with the untameable sea,[6] and alluded to the theme almost four decades later in his *I Chose Canada*. Observing that Canadian farmers had "coaxed millions of acres into smiling green meadows and prosperous fields," he contrasted this achievement with that of Newfoundlanders: "at the end of the first 400 years of toil, they had no productive meadows....For during those four centuries, their cultivation was of the unquiet, infuriate North Atlantic..., and all the toil and danger had not won an acre for them...."[7] Farley Mowat mused over the same contrast both in *Grey Seas Under* and in *This Rock Within the Sea*. On the theme of the tameless, untillable sea he quotes a wise old fisherman, "Ah, me son, we don't be *takin'* nothin' from the sea. We has to sneak up on what we wants, and wiggle it away."[8] The land can be tamed to man's purposes, but we cannot enclose and cultivate the seas. We are capelin fishermen casting our nets on wild, exposed beaches, casting between the breakers, ready always to dash for safety, ever looking over our shoulders for the yet more furious comber rolling in unobserved or poised to dash us against the rocks. He who casts his net must sneak up and wiggle his catch away.

But to till the soil, to enclose the land and year by year to improove it is to "over master the primordial and elemental forces" of land and sky. This was the advantage and the promise given in the dawn of the days to the first farmers.

> And the Lord God planted a garden eastward in Eden; and there he put the man whom he had formed. And a river went out of Eden to water the garden. And the Lord God took the man, and put him into the garden of Eden to dress it and keep it.

As a tiller of the soil, Adam had the power to appropriate and to possess it. But the fisherman cannot possess the sea. For him the stilling of the waters is a miracle.

> And there arose a great storm of wind, and the waves beat into the ship, so that it was now full. And they say unto him, Master, carest thou not that we perish? And he arose, and rebuked the wind, and said unto the sea. Peace, be still. And the wind ceased, and there was a great calm.

Is it any wonder that Peter was a man of little faith? And is it not fitting, nonetheless, that history has been kinder to him than to Adam?

The tiller of the soil "passes into the evening shadows as into rest." He turns his face homeward toward the setting of the sun with a sense of ownership. Having mixed his labours with the soil, he has a firm hope that on the morrow it will bear fruit, for himself and for "succeeding generations, without end." As Duncan noted in *The Way of the Sea*: "The tiller of the soil sows in peace, and in a yellow hazy peace he reaps; he passes his hand over a field, and, lo, in good season he gathers a harvest, for the earth rejoices to serve him."

If labours mark the labourers, Adam gained a sense of mastery over the great primordial forces and a consequent sense of inner freedom and control over his own destiny. Perhaps that is why he so quickly decided to take matters into his own hands and was banished from the garden. As a tiller of the soil, Adam was not simply a toiler, but a creator. And the more he created, the more his sense of control dominated his thinking.[9] But this sense of control and creativity does not come naturally to those who wrest their living from the ocean depths. The fisherman is not soon possessed of that pride and *hubris* which led to Adam's fall. The sea cannot be cultivated, nor can it be enclosed and brought into one's possession. In it there is no seed time and no assured harvest, and no part of it can be passed on to the next and succeeding generations. Man leaves no mark of his labours upon the sea. In the Old Testament language of Duncan's *The Way of the Sea*, the sea "groweth not old with the men who toil from its coasts. Generation upon the heels of generation...go forth in hope against it, continuing for a space, and returning spent to the dust." Recently I saw in a book of Irish photography a striking pastoral scene. An elderly man is standing on a hill, looking out over his farm in the fertile valley below. His dwelling is old, his land enclosed by fences of weathered stone; on his right hand is an ancient tree, and in front of him, shrubs yearly renewing themselves. For the hundredth time and perhaps for the thousandth the land had yielded its harvest, the grain or hay already raked into neat stacks on the harvest-brown field. It is the evening of the old farmer's day. And how telling the caption: "Generations."

As an encloser and possessor, the tiller of the soil can rest in the evening and behold the work of his hands and of his father's hands; and cast his eye over his children's inheritance. But it is not given to the fisherman to feel this deep sense of possession. No work of his hands can be passed on to his children. True he can build a new boat for next year. But, unlike the enduring hedges of stone and the tilled fields, that too is impermanent. It will soon spring a leak or go with the wind to feed what Pratt called "the primal hungers of a reef" ("The Ground Swell"), or, like Uncle Nick Top's *Shining Light*, fall prey to the teeth of an ice-pack. Thus it is interesting to contrast pastoral hymns with hymns of the sea. It is not accidental that pastoral hymns are hymns of thanksgiving. Thus:

Come, ye thankful people, come
Raise the song of harvest-home:
All is safely gathered in,
Ere the winter storms begin.

or

By Him the rolling seasons
In fruitful order move;
Sing to the Lord of harvest
A song of happy love.

But while the tiller of the soil lifts up his voice in praise for the bounties of his land, the fisherman, like Peter on Galilee, must pray for his very survival. "O hear us when we cry to Thee/For those in peril on the sea." Where the farmer sows in the appointed season, the fisherman must await a time. And when the time comes there is no assurance that the fish will be running." And Simon answering said unto him, Master, we have toiled all night, and have taken nothing." Simon's nets were filled only by a miracle. As Duncan so aptly put it in *Dr. Grenfell's Parish*, the fishery "is a great lottery of hope and fortune." It is not surprising, then, that the awaiting upon events which we cannot control, and the daily facing of primordial forces which we dare not defy, have coloured our outlook with the dark hues of fatalism.

It is surprising on first view that while the stormy North Atlantic was sculpturing into our souls dark caverns of fatalism, it was turning us into fighters, warrior vikings on the sea. Fatalism, however, is not a conviction that our dory will fail to make it, but a sense that it is beyond one's control whether she makes it or not. Fatalism permits of struggle and battle even though the outcome rests with the gods.

However difficult it is to reconcile this with our fatalism, we came to look upon the fishery, whether on the Grand Banks or the Labrador, whether at the Funks or at the Front, as a battle to be waged. The undertones of battle in our life on the sea have seized the imagination of a variety of observers. One of the first writers to note this was J.B. Jukes, an English geologist engaged by the Newfoundland government in 1839, whose curiosity led him to the ice in the *Topaz* in March 1840. One day when he had left the *Topaz* in a punt to participate in the kill he was revolted by the sight of slaughter and blood, and was seized with a desire to return immediately to the ship. But he was caught up in the battle cry. As he put it, "the hunting spirit which makes almost every man an animal of prey, and delight in the produce of his gun or bow, kept me in the punt till the late hour of the afternoon."[10] The same feature of the hunt was noted by Moses Harvey and Joseph Hatton in their *Newfoundland, The Oldest British Colony* (1883), the seal hunt depicted as "an army going out to do battle for those who remain at home", while the hunters come back "like returning conquerors." And in his *The Way of the Sea* Norman Duncan noted that "cod and salmon and seal-fat are the spoils of grim battles."

George Allan England, an American observer, best captured the spirit of battle in the seal fishery. His *Vikings of the Ice* is by far the best account of the seal hunt. On first sighting seals, he observed, "confusion burst like a shell." "Keen with blood lust, all who could go on ice began heaving on their gear. Such a shouting, such a leaping to arms, such a buckling-on of sheath knives, steels, belts; such a grabbing of tow ropes and murderous gaffs you could never imagine."[11] Young Cyril, a lad of sixteen, led the warriors over the side of the ship. "He led the leaping, yelling crowd that jumped to the loose-broken pans; that scrambled...to solid floes, and...ran like mad demons, yelling, across that fantastic confusion." Back on ship at night Uncle Edgar Tucker, under strong persuasion, cleared his throat and rhymed off seven verses of "Willy March", the first of which ran:

De home of his childhood, in Nothren Bay,
He quit it fer pleasure, much more 'an fer pay.
On de icefields he ventured, most yout'ful an' brave,
Whereon he sought death, but his life could not save.[12]

Of the writers who reported a spirit of battle in our approach to the sea, and in particular to the seal fishery, Farley Mowat is the last I shall mention. In his *Wake of the Great Sealers*, he reports a sealer's own explanation as to why men went to the ice in face of danger and for uncertain gain. "Oft-times I asks myself why we was so foolish. Perhaps it was like going off to the wars. Certainly there was risk enough and blood enough. It seemed like you weren't a proper man at all unless you'd gone to the ice...."[13]

Is it possible that our battle with what R.A. Parsons in "Salute to Port de Grave" calls our "beloved enemy the sea" has, paradoxically, induced in us resignation on the land, passivity in social and community affairs? It is not hard to imagine that while tillers of the soil naturally develop a positive and creative spirit, those who must go down to do battle with the sea are likely to become more negative and passive as citizens. What does the character of Pratt's Rachel reveal? Her practised eye on ominous clouds coming out of the dark west, the widow, having already lost father and husband to the sea's rage, waits alone through the long hours of her young son's first — and last — night at sea "her long thin fingers intertwined/And resting on her lap."[14] Passively waiting on the will of forces beyond her control, was not Rachel one of us? And is it possible that this passive and stoic philosophy is reflected in our social and political attitudes? Certainly active efforts to plan communities and to establish for that purpose town councils were few indeed until the years immediately following Confederation. And when town councils did spring up, were they not the artificial creations of a "centralist" government? The question I am suggesting for future treatment by poet and novelist is whether our battles with the sea have not, surprisingly, turned us into mystics and stoics on the land.

Certainly more than one writer has raised the thought. In an article written in 1937, J.R. Smallwood put it as clearly as any. "Perhaps," he wrote, "the very nature of our struggle, of our methods of wresting a living from Nature, has helped to unfit us for creative and constructive effort."

> It is a fact that for centuries we have lived by *killing* cod and other fish; by *killing* seals in the water or on the ice, and animals on the land; by *killing* birds, and *cutting down* trees. Has all this developed in us a trait of destructiveness, or narcotised what ought actually to be an instinct of creativeness?"[15]

Richard Gwyn in his study of Smallwood quotes this striking passage, concluding that our "struggle for survival exhausted ambition and creativity."[16] I believe, however, that it was not struggle as such that marked us; but the kind of struggle, a tearing down, a 'killing', in contrast to the farmer's building up, growing and cultivating; the snatching of our daily food from a hostile environment. In expressing puzzlement as to why

Newfoundlanders, a people "given to storytelling, warmly appreciative of song and verse, the turn of a phrase", had not produced more creative writers, Ebbitt Cutler, Editor of the *Greatest Hunt in the World*, also quotes Smallwood's passage, and concludes that killing "as a substitute for creativeness is certainly relevant."

And why was it true, as J.R. Smallwood observed in *I Chose Canada*, that after four hundred years we had "precious few substantial houses?" Is it possible that our poverty alone cannot explain this? Did lack of means prevent us from erecting buildings on more secure foundations, did lack of money prevent us from taking elementary steps to keep window curtains from spreading like sails on a windy night; and why were our fish-flakes always about to collapse on their rickety legs? Approached from seaward, our fishing villages, our dwellings, flakes and stages, and even our roads, present an air of impermanence. Like the fishing-stations of Black Jo, Fichot Islands and Pillar Bight, they seem to have been erected for a season, the expectation of imminent abandonment built into their flimsy structures. As one's boat approaches Cook's Harbour, Shoe Cove or Stocking Harbour the impression deepens that the name 'fishing-station' would most accurately describe the scene before him.

He might suddenly be struck by the fact, and think it not unnatural, that in Newfoundland these outports, these clusters of houses, are not referred to as villages by local people. I am suggesting that the explanation of this atmosphere of impermanence lies less in our economics than in our souls. For it is not far-fetched to suggest that a life-long battler on the sea, a fish killer, will be a less than enthusiastic planner, creator and builder ashore.

For it may be that the fisherman's dwelling does not serve the same purposes as the farmer's. He does not envisage generations inheriting his dwelling as they inherit the durable homes, the stone hedges and the tilled soil; his house is a roof over his head. His time is the time of his own life and of his children's while they are young. For him past time does not flow over into the future as it must do for the settled farmer. Time is not arrested in the hills or in his home's firm foundations, or in the stone hedges and ancient trees; it is an ever-rolling stream. Unlike the farmer he lacks a deep sense of the permanence of things. That is why I felt it not untrue to suggest, in another place; that a Newfoundlander is "a person who dwells between the beginning and the end, who has one eye fixed on history and the other on eschatology."

Turning now to a last question about the sea and our souls, it has been suggested that our encounters with ocean storms, as representations of primordial laws admitting of no alteration and of no tampering by man, has profoundly affected our religious sensibilities. On the purely intellectual level, perhaps one would be surprised to find belief in any extraneous forces among people to whom nature presents her face as a cosmos of iron-clad law. Yet it is on a deeper level natural that a North Atlantic fishing people should find a place for powers and agencies outside nature itself. For whereas the great forces of nature, the rampaging flood, the raging tempest, the over-powering Alps, viewed with detachment from afar, that is from a safe vantage point, appeal to the artist in us, and are called sublime; seen in terms of their effects, as threats to our very existence, they evoke in us fear and dread. And that is why we so naturally personify them, why capricious and malignant forces are but the other side of nature. As Thomas Crewe of Finger Cove observed, "the wind is the hand o' the Lard, without pity and wonderful for strength."[17] The people of Ragged Harbour on the night of the great storm "wondered what the Lord God Almighty intended." It was only natural, then, that Billy Luff became converted on the very night "when the vibrant voice [of the minister] was lifted above a gusty night wind and the roar of the Black Rock breakers."[18] Thus where the laws of nature threaten man, it is natural that he should personify them.

How far beneath the surface of our sea hymns is the terrible, personified side of nature? The tiller of the soil affirms his being led into green pastures, beside the still waters. But what the night wind carries from the lips of the mariner is always a question, and the question is never answered until the anchor is cast and the sail furled. "Oh hear us when we cry to Thee." To the Newfoundlander the stilling of the waters of Galilee is the most surprising and most satisfying of miracles.

Are the gods of the sea less to be loved than propitiated and sometimes defied? May they not be harsher than pastoral gods? Is this what Duncan meant by the statement that the untamable ocean robs "souls of their graces", and by this striking passage from *The Way of the Sea*?

> When they (fishermen from the bleak coast) roam afar — as from bleak places, where no yellow fields, no broad, waving acres, yielding bounteously, make love manifest to the children of men..., when they roam afar, it may be, the gods they fetch back are terrible gods.

Perhaps our religion reflects more the might of the seas than the fertility of the land. Certainly in Ragged Harbour and Twist Tickle souls are stirred less by the promise of green pastures than by the majesty of the restless wave. And "a great whirlwind shall be raised up from the coasts of the earth. The Lord hath his way in the whirlwind and in the storm." In Ragged Harbour, "some men have fashioned a god of rock and tempest and the sea's rage — a gigantic, frowning shape, throned in a mist, whereunder black waters curl and hiss, and are cold and without end."[19]

Perhaps we personify the terrible by a psychological law, some law of our nature as iron-clad and unalterable as the laws of sea and the wind. For when threatening forces are personified the battle becomes personal and the hope for victory a little more realistic. The sailor's belief in jinkers illustrates this law of our nature. In his book *Forty-Eight Days Adrift* Captain Job Barbour discusses the jinker. A jinker, as this seasoned mariner wrote, "is a member of a ship's crew who is believed always to bring bad luck." "Of one thing I am certain," Barbour says, "and that is that all sailors and fishermen believe in the malign influence of the jinker and fear him."[20] Barbour himself professes to be willing to leave the question of the truth of this belief to readers, but in telling how five years before he shipped a jinker on the *Sea Bird* and was immediately battered by a hurricane he confesses: "Of course, I was responsible in the eyes of the crew for having taken the jinker on board and I punished myself and kept clear of their accusing looks by holding the wheel for eleven consecutive hours." Was Barbour driven to this measure by fear of the crew only? On a ship the jinker soon becomes responsible for the demons of the storm, and can be dismissed from his duties, sent below for the duration of the voyage, his powers nullified; or, in the extremity, he can be cast into the midst of the sea. "But the Lord sent out a great wind into the sea, and there was a mighty tempest...so that the ship was like to be broken." Then the sailors were afraid and said everyone to his fellow, "Come let us cast lots, that we may know for whose cause this evil is upon us." And they cast lots and "took up Jonah, and cast him forth into the sea: and the sea ceased from her raging."

We have not only jinkers, but ghosts. Why are there more ghosts per harbour and cove in Newfoundland than anywhere else in North America? Is it unnatural that a people as bound and confined by the laws of nature as they were confined on the close of navigation should envisage a place for beings subject to none of these limitations? Or, far from being unnatural, is it inevitable that such a people would make room for free spirits as the Epicureans left spaces for their gods in a universe that was otherwise but matter in motion? Perhaps these are questions to which the dark sides of our souls will yield no answer. In any case we delight — even when our nerves tingle — in the sight of ghosts and spirits breaking all of the laws that so confine us and so often take on the countenance of enemies. So much the worse for the laws of nature when a ghost at one and the same time can be seen in Julie's Harbour and boarding a boat at anchor in Hussey's Cove; when wingless it can defy gravitation, or appear as a ball of fire on the crest of a wave. Do ghosts take upon themselves our impotence as the scapegoat took our sins into the desert?

The carved and rugged headlands of this sea-worn rock witness to the might and fury of the tempest. The marks it has made on our souls are as deep, and perhaps as abiding, as the seams in the granite cliff. As my little tribute to that son of Newfoundland whose words so beautifully caught the voice of the sea, I end with these lines from Pratt.[21]

> Tell me thy secret, O Sea,
>   The mystery sealed in thy breast;
> Come, breathe it in whispers to me,
>   A child of thy fevered unrest.

Cyril F. Poole

Notes

1. Farley Mowat and John de Visser. *This Rock Within the Sea: A Heritage Lost*. Toronto: Little, Brown and Co., 1968. n.p.

2. "Death of an Outport", *Baffles of Wind and Tide*, ed. Clyde Rose. Breakwater Books, 1974, p.63.

3. *Salute to Port de Grave*. Don Mills: The Ontario Publishing Co., 1975, p.21.

4. Norman Duncan. *The Way of the Sea*. New York: McClure, Phillips & Co., 1903, pp.309-10.

5. *Dr. Grenfell's Parish*. New York: Fleming H. Revell Co., 1906, pp. 121-127.

6. "Newfoundland To-day", *The Book of Newfoundland*, Vol. 1, 1937, p.1.

7. *I Chose Canada.* Toronto: Macmillan of Canada, 1973, p.10.

8. *Grey Seas Under.* Ballantine Books, Inc. 1958, p.21.

9. In his Convocation Address at Memorial University, December 3, 1977, Dr. Leslie Harris presented an extraordinarily perceptive analysis of man's *hubris* attendant on his ability to master his environment. The Address was later published in the M.U.N. *Gazette*, Vol. 10, No.8.

10. *Excursions in and about Newfoundland.* London: John Murray, 1842, reprinted by Canadiana House, 1969, Vol. 1, p. 291.

11. *Vikings of the Ice.* 1924; republished by Tundra Books, Inc., 1969, under the title *The Greatest Hunt in the World,* p. 82.

12. *The Greatest Hunt in the World,* p.126.

13. Farley Mowat. *Wake of the Great Sealers.* Prints and drawings by David Blackwood. Toronto: McClelland and Stewart, 1973, p.57.

14. "Rachel", *Here the Tides Flow,* ed. D.G. Pitt, Toronto: Macmillan and Co. of Canada, 1962, p.53.

15. J.R. Smallwood. "Newfoundland To-day." *The Book of Newfoundland,* Vol.1, p.1.

16. Richard Gwyn. *Smallwood: The Unlikely Revolutionary.* Toronto: McClelland and Stewart, 1969, p. XII.

17. Norman Duncan. *The Way of the Sea,* p.260.

18. *Ibid.* p.131.

19. *Ibid.* p.220.

20. Job Kean Barbour. *Forty-Eight Days Adrift.* London: R. Clay and Sons, 1932, p.5. [new edition: Breakwater Books, 1981.]

21. E.J. Pratt. "The Secret of the Sea", *Here the Tides Flow,* ed. D.G. Pitt, Toronto: The Macmillan Co. of Canada, 1962.

Dr. Cyril F. Poole was born in Pilley's Island, Notre Dame Bay, Newfoundland. He is presently Principal of Sir Wilfred Grenfell College, Corner Brook. His close association with the sea and with education are both reflected in this essay. His wit and writing skill are evidenced in *The Time of My Life* and *In Search of the Newfoundland Soul.* He was the first winner of the Newfoundland and Labrador Arts Council's Award for Humour.

Questions

1. How does the author show that Newfoundlanders have a sense of fatalism juxtaposed with a spirit of battle.

2. People who "do battle with the sea are likely to become more negative and passive as citizens". How does Dr. Poole arrive at that conclusion?

3. Do you agree with the author that "this atmosphere of impermanence" found among our people and our communities "lies less in our economics than in our souls"? Why or why not?

4. Point of view colors the tone of an essay. What is the tone of this essay and how has the author's point of view enhanced it?

5. There are many, many references to other writers and other works in this essay. Do these references detract from or add to the effectiveness of the points being made? Support your answer.

Activities

1. Debate: Be it resolved that ambition and creativity have been stifled in the Newfoundland people because their lives have centered on the sea.

2. Notice the parallels between Norman Duncan's story at the beginning of the unit and Dr. Poole's essay. Discuss these parallels.

3. Ask your Newfoundland culture teacher or your history teacher about our social and political attitudes in this province over the years. Have they reflected a "passive and stoic philosophy" as suggested by the author?

4. See if you can find any Newfoundland paintings or photographs of the sea which show it as calm and serene. Contrast these with ones of the opposite type.

5. Make a tape of hymns of the sea. Listen to them with the class. Do the hymns reflect the "terrible, personified nature" mentioned by Dr. Poole? Perhaps you'd like to get a grandparent or a senior citizen friend to sing these hymns for you to tape. That will add some Newfoundland soul to your project.

6. Use a good dictionary to check the etymologies of hubris, Epicurean, and eschatology.

7. For more information on "jinker" refer to *The Dictonary of Newfoundland English*, Story, Kirwin, Widdowson.

8. The fatalism found in "Riders to the Sea" by J.M. Synge in *Dramatic Literature* lends further support to Poole's theories regarding people of the sea. Read it.

This Dear and Fine Country — Spina Sanctus

Well, we made it once again, boys!

Winter is over.

Oh, but there is still snow on the ground.

So what? It hasn't got a chance. It is living in jeopardy from day to day. We should pity it because it will soon be ready for the funeral parlour.

It is only a matter of another few paltry weeks and we shall see it disappear into brown and foaming brooks; we shall see the meadows burning green and spangled with little piss-a-beds like tiny yellow suns.

Winter is over.

Oh, but there is still ice in the water.

So what? The globe is turning and nothing can stop it.

We are revolving into light.

The fisherman tars his boat on the beach and is heated by two suns, one in the sky and another reflected from the water, and the ice on the cliff behind him drips away to a poor skeleton.

It is only a matter of a few more paltry weeks and we shall see the steam rising from the ponds and from the damp ground behind the plow; we shall see the grandmothers sitting out by the doorstep for a few minutes watching the cat; we shall see the small boats a'bustle, piled high with lobster pots in the bow, and the days melting further and further into the night.

Winter is over now.

Praise God and all honour to our forefathers through generations who did never forsake this dear and fine Country.

Ray Guy

A biographical note on the author is to be found on page 23.

UNIT 2

Ocean and Outport

Ocean and Outport

Love of place is a theme which is common in the literature of all countries. It seems that there is really no place quite as full of contentment as the place where one is born and reared. In days gone by it was not unusual for a person to spend practically a lifetime in the same community. Today we are experiencing a much more mobile lifestyle, so that even when we want to stay in one place such things as transfers, changing economic conditions, opportunities for advancement, and the ease of transportation make moving more acceptable. But for people who have established generations of occupation in a particular area a move can be a traumatic experience. For many people in Newfoundland this happened during the resettlement period of the sixties and seventies. But the trauma associated with resettlement is not unique to this province. The people of Latvia, Lithuania and Estonia moved en masse to parts of the Soviet Union. The Crofters were moved from the Scottish Highlands, and the Irish left a famine stricken country to come to North America. In all these situations there were anguish and heartbreak. There are few loves stronger than the love of people for their "place". Yet one stronger love is the love of parents for their children. We find strong expression of these loves in much of the literature associated with these movements, a sense of longing or yearning for the place left, and anger at the circumstances which made the move necessary, balanced by the understanding that the move will benefit the young.

There is a strong sense of place in these writings. The geographic region helps shape the characters, and the interaction of place and people produces dominant qualities that become characteristic of the literature, its mood and images.

Thus, in Ron Pollett's descriptive essay, "The Ocean at My Door", the Newfoundland house becomes large, tough, and dominating — proud to stand "four square" against the mighty Atlantic Ocean — subtly suggesting that these are the characteristics of the people. In Tom Dawe's lyrical poem "Abandoned Outport", the beauty of the landscape is emphasized to suggest the quiet, peaceful nature of the outporters. In "Moving Day" Helen Porter questions the validity of the claim that geography has such hold on the people; it is true that the mother weeps most on the day the settlers abandon the island, but it is also she who insists that isolation is a curse. Geraldine Rubia's "Leave-Taking" is a symbolic demonstration that the strong forces which call people to an almost worshipful love of their roots is matched by an equal force which calls them to move on to new challenges and places — the very force which perhaps beckoned people to leave the old world and settle the new. Horwood and Pittman use the nature and fate of the outports as jumping-off places to interesting explorations of place, people and philosophies.

Each selection is introduced by a headnote. The headnote is a possible interpretation of the theme in the selection, but is also a challenge. Let each headnote make you think, but do not let it make your thinking.

This descriptive essay is an impressionistic account of the inside of a large old-fashioned Newfoundland house built near the Atlantic Ocean. Typically, the kitchen is the center of attraction, not only for the family and friends downstairs but for the children upstairs who listened as "conversation climbed with the lamplight along the funnel." The chimney and its three stoves epitomize the old Newfoundland outport life itself: kitchen stove for everyone, parlor stove for special guests, a small upstairs stove for the parents' bedroom, a chimney in a bedroom a child was lucky to get and must lose when an old grandparent became ill enough to want permanent bedrest and regular heat. Nor are other parts of the house's great insides neglected: the large back porch for everyday entry and storage, the hallway for convenient access to upstairs, the stairs with banisters and balustrade for youthful gymnastics, the small front porch to get rid of front-door drafts, and the parlor for special visits. Throughout the essay, with vivid diction and an excellent command of recalled firsthand experience, the essayist presents masterfully, almost personifies, the old Newfoundland home beside the sea. In a very subtle way, too, he suggests how important home roots were to those people who are now east coast Canadians.

The Ocean At My Door

The day I was born my father was so happy to have a son he bought me a suit the same afternoon. Almost fifty years later, when he was pushing ninety, I bought him a suit, which he promptly put aside "to be buried in." I had to wait several years before I could wear my suit and it looks as though it will be some time yet before he wears his.

That's how it usually is with Newfoundlanders: they are born very young and die very old. And my father is not the only one to live all his life with a weather eye peeled to the future.

This big day in the life of my father was at the beginning of the century. It was a big day for me too, because it is the best time to begin the first hundred years — right on the button. In all my lifetime it has never been necessary that I know arithmetic in order to reckon my age, for the figures come out in print every year on the current calendar. Even when no calendar is in sight I can never be stuck so long as I know what year it is.

● ● ●

I was the third child in a family of seven. There were only seven children because my mother got a late start and because nature spaced us three or four years apart. My paternal grandmother went ten better although handicapped by having to sit out mourning periods after burying

57

three husbands — one at a time, of course. At that, seventeen was a bit better than the average even in those times. The old woman lived almost a hundred years. I was sixteen when she died.

• • •

The first air into my lungs was the salty ozone from the north Atlantic Ocean. Our house was so near the water that if I had been born in blustery weather I would have been christened with spray long before I reached the arms of the minister. Every fall the swift fingers of the ocean in the first big blow of the season obligingly wiped away the summer's crop of fly specks on the outside of our front windows, leaving in its place a smudgy residue that glittered in the sun until winter. And in winter the panes were almost permanently encrusted with frost from icy winds off the frozen bay.

As it happened, I started with the bright and balmy days of early summer so was able to gain a firm toehold against the rigours of coming seasons. All I had to survive as my mother bounced me around in the sunshine, visiting in the village, were the horny-fingered admiration of relatives and neighbours and the ravages of hungry mosquitoes and other stinging insects we encountered on the way. I must have done all right too, because when I was baptized that fall my wails topped the peals of the church organ as I waited in a rear pew for the end of the regular service. My father squared his shoulders when one of my Godfathers remarked after the ceremony:

"You've got a strong feller there, Jim. Nothing better than a boy who can holler. He'll be manning the for'rd oar in no time."

And he didn't mean the for'rd oar at Oxford or Yale!

I was suckled at my mother's breast, as were all our family. That was the custom as well as the necessity of the times. It was an intimate custom that fostered the warmth and love every child has a right to expect and at the same time provided the correct milk formula without my mother ever knowing the meaning of the word. I, therefore, had an old-fashioned start, and it was a good, healthy push.

I was four years old and my brother had just been born when we moved into our new house nearby. The old house was turned over to the livestock — the downstairs a stable, the upstairs a hayloft.

• • •

The new house was larger - much larger. It was even nearer the water than was the old place and it stood bolt and solid as if challenging the ocean. And braver still, it faced the north. Tall fir trees and hardy spruces with spreading thick branches crowded guard at the rear, but at the right was only a small bare hill over which the chill, damp east winds zoomed to hit the roof. The warm west winds and sunshine had a clear path over a meadow. In spring and fall the gable roof cast a long shadow on the slope of the hill.

As is customary in Newfoundland village homes, the main entrance to our house was at the rear. It was through a long, enclosed porch partitioned in half to make a storeroom at the other end. Straight ahead was the big kitchen, with the dining room offside at the right in a wing. A

58

door at the far end of the kitchen opened to a hallway that ran through to the front porch. On the left in the hall was the parlour entrance, the stairway on the right. The small front porch led to the verandah, which fronted the parlour. Only important visitors were ushered in at the front.

The verandah was a nice place summertime to sit and watch the harbour and the boats and otherwise keep in touch with things. The main road that skirted the landwash around the village ran by so near we could hear what the passers-by were saying and almost see the colour of their eyes. The verandah made a splendid perch for anyone who liked company.

But I wasn't old enough then to be interested in the landscape. What got my attention, after I had finished exploring the dark cubbyhole underneath the stairway, was the big kitchen. In the old house the kitchen was small but here there was room for Gran's rocking chair between the cradle in a corner and the big stove at the centre near a wall. I would make a beeline for that cradle whenever I saw it empty and would ask Gran to rock me and sing about the river. The song she sang was "Shall we gather at the river, the beautiful, the beautiful river..." She sang it over and over, rocking the cradle all the while. It was a pretty soft racket for me.

I stuck to the cradle until I outgrew it. But by that time my brother had heard about the river and took up where I left off. Gran had a steady job.

The house had straight stairs with banisters and a balustrade down which I could slide. In the old place the stairway was winding and cramped and had only a thin rail. But I soon tired of the stairs and asked my father to put in a ladder instead. The reason was, I had stayed overnight in a house that had a ladder for going upstairs and I thought that more fun. There was adventure in climbing a ladder.

● ● ●

I slept in the room over the kitchen. In winter this was the coziest place upstairs because the stove pipe, called a "funnel," ran through to the roof. The wall near the funnel was inlaid with tin sheathing as were the floor and ceiling around the holes where the pipe entered and left. On bitterly cold nights the funnel got red hot in places and the tin back radiated heat as from the sun. The goatskin rug near the bed retained this heat as if awaiting my bare feet when I got out of bed. Things could have been worse.

Here a few years later is where I taught my brother the fascinating pastime called "Who Can Keep His Hand on the Hot Funnel the Longest?" This game is easy to learn but hard to play, and more than once my mother hollered up to inquire why my brother was crying.

"He burned his hand on the hot funnel again," I would answer through the opening around the flange where the light shone through from the kitchen.

This lighthouse beam from downstairs was a year-round comfort in the dark room after bedtime. When there were visitors the kitchen (which was also the living-room) buzzed with voices, and snatches of conversation climbed with the lamplight along the funnel. Long before radio was invented I had cocked my ears to what must have been choice bits of local news and gossip from this loudspeaker, but I wasn't old eough then to know what it was all about. And by the time I got old enough there was no more funnel.

The chimney that replaced it was to me a cold and impartial thing. It came, along with other improvements, the year my father had an extra prosperous season. I watched the mason pattycake the mortar on to the bricks and was greatly taken at the way he captured the oozings with a deft turn of the trowel. He was as smart as a whip. He chewed tobacco and spat into the dark hole, which I thought a good place to spit.

Two stoves were installed with the chimney. The one upstairs in my parents' room was tiny indeed and could burn only the smallest kind of wood billets. That first winter the stove was lit every evening just before dark. My mother let me kindle the fire and I made the chokies with my own pocket-knife. My father said I made the best shavings he ever saw.

• • •

The other stove was in the front room downstairs - the parlor. It was a heating stove about half the size of the big one in the kitchen. It had bright-plated buffers, a shiny grilled top piece that swung on a swivel, and the door was panelled with mica. I wondered why this mica stuff didn't catch fire and burn, since the flames danced 'round it and it certainly looked fragile. I began to explore. In no time I had a hole picked through. I told my father I busted it putting in a junk of wood. But I got a lacing just the same.

When the three stoves were going full blast together a pillar of smoke poured from the chimney and on calm days spiralled far into the sky before curling away into nothing. I used to brag about the lot of smoke our chimney made compared to the thin dribble from houses that still had funnels.

For me, everything seemed to revolve around the chimney, and the year must have been a memorable one for the rest of the family as well. That fall saw a new leather couch and two upholstered chairs in the parlour. A new oblong table stood firmly in the centre of the room. It was covered with a tapestry cloth that had a big ball fringe all around. The shade on the new table lamp was bordered with glass crystals that tinkled when the lamp was moved and reflected the light in colours. It looked pretty. On Sunday mornings after breakfast my father would lie on the couch and sleep until noon. But we children saw very little of the parlour.

• • •

About this time my father broke out with a "corky" hat — a bowler — which he wore on Sunday afternoons in summer. He seemed to be ever so proud of the hat. He and the other men in the village always were togged off on Sunday afternoons. His necktie had a built-in knot with ears that fitted into the high celluloid collar, and a wire hook that fastened on the stud. The hat created some awe among us children because it was kept in a box upstairs all week and was never hung on the wall or left lying around like a cap. On occasions when my father laid it on the parlor table I often tried the hat on and even blew hard into the air holes on the sides, but they wouldn't whistle. The hat was black and couldn't show handling, but my mother cautioned me not to make dents.

One day, however, I left it on a chair. No, nobody sat on it; but the cat chose this opportunity to start sharpening her claws and had worried quite a nap spot on the crown before I caught her. I was scared, but my mother fixed it with a damp cloth and a tiny dab of shoe polish, and my father never knew the difference.

I was to sleep in the room with the chimney only one year. Gran had now taken to her bed for good and was moved into this room where it was warmer. She had a brand-new iron bedstead with metal slats and a new feather mattress. The bed had casters on the bottom and brass knobs on top of the corner rods.

My brother and I soon discovered that these knobs could be unscrewed and we took them off and put them back on a thousand times. Finally they became so loose they jingled like bells every time Gran moved. But my grandmother was hard of hearing as well as blind, so it didn't make any difference.

It was here, sitting on the bed, I listened to Gran tell many wonderful yarns about pioneer days on the Avalon Peninsula. She could gab all day when there was anyone to listen. When there was nobody, she would sing and pray and sing and pray. I asked her why she prayed so much and she said she was talking to God for company.

* * *

Gran was ninety now. She was to live seven more long years — all of them in that bed.

My brother and I were moved into a tiny room off to one side at the front where the window faced the sea. The older sisters were given Gran's old place in the wing, over the dining room. We called our cubicle the Bird's Nest. It had northern exposure — and "exposure" is the correct word. In winter it was so cold our breaths formed hoar frost on the bedclothes so that we woke up wearing white whiskers. Even the goatskin rug that was so warm in the other room was like ice to my bare feet here.

Those were old-time winters that lasted from November until March, with snow heaped high and sub-zero temperatures prevailing. The hot bricks we took to bed and the piled-up bedclothes and our young blood kept us from freezing. Years later when I heard a joke on the radio about it being so cold up North the blankets on the bed fought one another trying to get on the bottom, I thought of that room.

We had the same old wooden bed with rope "netting" to hold up the mattress, which was a cotton-duck sack stuffed with eelgrass. We called the grass "grays" because gray was the colour when it dried. It was comfortable enough and had a healthy smell like seaweed. But we boys were the only ones left out in the cold without a feather bed the year father hit it "rich."

The pillows were feather-stuffed and downy. That was something we had new. I told my brother the feathers were special ones from underneath the wings of the wild ducks and that if he listened hard enough he would hear the ducks flying. He listened and listened until finally he could hear the ducks, he said.

When he reported this downstairs my mother looked at him hard and wrinkled her forehead. I knew that to be a bad sign, when she wrinkled her forehead. We were all at the supper table. I had no choice but to explain although I hated to spoil a good thing by talking out loud about it.

"No, there's nothing the matter with his head," I said, "I'm the one who put it in his mind. Anyhow, he's at the age he'd believe anything," I added importantly.

The others laughed but my mother still frowned. Then she smiled too. She probably remembered she had gone through the same kind of thing herself, as a little girl, putting a seashell to her ear and hearing the waves roar inside the shell.

Now that there was no longer a funnel to play with, I soon invented a game much less hazardous but almost as exciting. This was called "Keeping the Feather in the Air." We each picked a tiny feather from the pillow and blew it in the air. The one whose feather touched anything lost the game. The ceiling was low and the trick was to use only a zephyr breath. I let my brother win once in a while. We played feathers a long time.

But the thing that had both of us puzzled was the wall-paper on the Bird's Nest. This was not ordinary paper as on the other rooms — no red roses or other coloured flowery designs to be looked at and promptly forgotten — but something special that required a lot of deep thought. It even required a name, so we called it the Running Boy and Racing Dog.

We could never make head or tail of this paper. It started off at the door-facing with a vertical panel of racing puppies. The next panel was a string of running boys; then the puppies again and so on. This continued all around the walls beside the bed, the puppies chasing the boys at a terrific pace until they reached the window. And here's where the trouble started. For when the race was stopped by the window the puppies were definitely in the lead! Where and how they passed the boys was what puzzled us, and the more we tried to figure this out the madder we got.

But there it was for anyone to see; the puppies were behind at the beginning of the race and ahead at the end.

In the years to come I was to see many odd patterns of wallpaper, but none to equal the enigma of the running boys.

(I was to sleep in that room with the northern exposure, in the same old wooden bed, until I grew into a young man and set out on my own. In the meantime, the many interesting things that happened in our family life and out into the wonderful world of this colourful Newfoundland outport — around the wharves, in the boats, at school, and among the woods and streams — would make a long, long story.)

Ron Pollett
(from *The Ocean at my Door*)

Ron Pollett was born in New Harbour, Trinity Bay, in 1900. He was a printer by trade but spent some time as a teacher. He moved to New York to pursue his career in printing, and while there he wrote much of his better known material. His love for Newfoundland is often clearly expressed as he used outport subjects for most of his work. His short story "The Born Trouter" is equivalent in mood to Yates' poem "Lake Isle of Innisfree". His writing is best known through his book *The Ocean at My Door*, and stories published in *The Atlantic Guardian*, a magazine which he helped to create, and which was incorporated into *The Atlantic Advocate*.

Questions

1. How are adjectives used effectively in this essay? Illustrate your answer with examples.

2. In a well-illustrated paragraph for each, show how the essay builds gradually in detail by referring to (a) different parts of the big house's insides (b) incidental references to the boyhood activities in the house.

3. State and illustrate three points about the ocean made by the essayist. How is each helpful in understanding the home roots of the outport Newfoundlanders?

4. How is the following appropriate as an expression of the essay's main theme: "The Newfoundland outport really only had five buildings: church, grocery shop, school, stage, and house. Of these, the house was by far the most important."?

5. How does the essayist associate his own home with the Newfoundland people? In a short, well-written paragraph, explain this idea. Use references as needed.

Activities

1. Family albums and public archives have photos of old colonial Newfoundland homes. Try to obtain several such photos, particularly ones with pictures of the insides of the homes. See how many details of the essay you can identify in the photos.

2. Read, at least twice, selections from Farley Mowat's *The Boat Who Wouldn't Float* and from Harold Horwood's *Newfoundland*. Write a review of each piece you read. Include parallels and differences between the pictures of Newfoundland life given by Mowat, Horwood, and Pollett.

3. Read several other essays about interesting happenings in family life in the home. Prepare an anthology on the subject of family life in Canadian literature. Illustrate your anthology with pictures from magazines and your own drawings and paintings.

4. "The problem with most Newfoundland writers is that they present the quaint and the old. They present Newfoundland as a place of codfish drying in the sun, with cod's liver decomposing in topless wooden barrels, men hauling codtraps, and women stringing caplin onto nails sticking out of racks. It would be an improvement if Newfoundland writers presented snowmobiles hauling *smuts* (firewood dried by a forest fire), airplanes climbing through the fog, men driving treefarmers, and women lobbying for changes in the Matrimonial Property Act." To what extent is this criticism a valid condemnation of Pollett's "The Ocean at My Door"? What changes would a modern writer put in an essay about a modern Newfoundland home?

Nature has always been a favourite theme for English poets and particularly so from the time of Wordsworth in the late eighteenth century up to the present time. Nature, it seems, is an outward manifestation that sets the inner spirits of our poets aglow. Tom Dawe is a nature poet in this tradition. His poem, "Abandoned Outport", is a classic response of wonder and sadness at the day and night beauty of a landscape that has been abandoned by the settlers who once lived on it and loved it. Notice the Haiku structure, and that the poem is cradled by the sun and the moon.

Abandoned Outport

Sun on boarded windows
and gull-cries
high in the August clouds.

On a small beach-path:
blue-bells nodding
over driftwood.

A bee is buzzing
inside dark cracks
in a window pane.

Clover meadow:
above the rusting ploughshare
a butterfly.

A sudden fog
and sea-winds
bend the sting-nettle.

Deep in graveyard grass
snails and lichens
cling to the headstone.

Across the schoolhouse floor:
paper scraps, dry sea-weed
and a dead moth.

Against the cold twilight:
dark picket-fences
and a crow's flight.

In a rising moon:
a church steeple
and lilac leaves.

Tom Dawe

Born in Manuels, Tom Dawe first displayed his literary talents in collaboration with Tom Moore in a book called *Connections*. In 1972 he was awarded the Elizabeth Burton Poetry Prize. In 1973 he won a special gold medal for visual arts in the Newfoundland Arts and Letters Competition. His important works are: *Hemlock Cove and After, In a Small Cove, Landwash Days, Island Spell, The Loon in the Dark Tide, A Gommil from Bumble Bee Bight*.

Questions

1. Why does the poet not mention the lilac leaves until he has set the sun?

2. Does this poem remind one more of the natural beauty of the outport than of the settlers' having abandoned it? Explain.

3. What is the poet's own personal response to the landscape? Can you guess from this how he feels about the people who have abandoned the outport?

4. How does Dawe remind us that people once lived in this outport? Give two quotations from the poem to support your answer. What do these quotations suggest about his attitude towards resettlement?

5. Using your own ideas, tell why this poem has meaning for many Newfoundlanders today.

Activities

1. Prepare a dramatic reading, either by yourself or with several classmates, of "Abandoned Outport". Accompany the reading with music.

2. In addition to those in this unit, find several other Newfoundland poems about resettlement. Prepare a tape-recording of your selections in which students introduce each poem, read it, and comment upon its main theme.

3. Prepare a class program about resettlement to which you invite your parents or another group of people. Include the following:

a. Narrator who introduces poems, stories, and other materials collected about your theme.

b. Readers and actors who dramatize what the narrator has introduced.

Hints: Songs and skits composed by students and teachers add immediacy and interest. Overhead transparencies to illustrate points make your work more memorable. Visitors who know from experience about resettlement will enliven your program.

4. Find at least one enjoyable nature poem written by each of the following famous writers: Wordsworth, Emerson, Thoreau, Whitman, Pratt. To what extent, judging simply by "Abandoned Outport", can Dawe be said to be a poetic brother of these great poets?

In this selection Harold Horwood combines the talents of nature writer, historian, social critic and analyst. The area which is the topic of the article is the Great Northern Peninsula of the island of Newfoundland. It will be helpful to have a good map of the island nearby for close consultation as the piece is read. An additional aid would be some of the several available books of photographs. Students should be aware that Wilfred Grenfell devoted his life's work to the people he met on this part of the coast. It is part of the "French Shore" and thus one of the last parts of the province to be settled. In several ways it was for years a representation of the old Newfoundland. To many Newfoundlanders it is still virtually unknown.

Transition

If you climb the head above Englee on a clear day in summer and turn your face to the slow-breathing Atlantic, you will see far away on your starboard bow the blue shapes of the Horse Islands like peaks against the faint line of the Burlington Peninsula. Ten miles ahead and to port are the massive Grey Islands, with the little peninsulas of Conche and Crouse laying close inshore. Beyond are Croque and St. Julien's and the Fichot Islands. Behind you lies the splendid fjord of Canada Bay. Far off on the starboard quarter to the southwest lie Hooping Harbour and cliff-ringed Williamsport and the splendid haven of Harbour Deep.

The men who watch the sea along this shore know all these places well. Their fathers and their grandfathers were born upon the islands and in the coves that dot the fjords along this awesome coast. There they grew to manhood in boats that now lie rotting, the sand clogging their guts and the stars shining between their ribs.

The silver flash of salmon in a hundred streams lured men westward from Bonavista into Notre Dame Bay, thence on into White Bay and down the eastern shore of the Great Northern Peninsula. So abundant was this superb fish a century ago that the men of Exploits and Green Bay and Sop's Arm and Harbour Deep were known to the rest of Newfoundland as "the salmon-catchers." They fished in the fjords with nets, and built wiers across the rivers to take the salmon on their upstream migration to the spawning beds. They salted them and smoked them and shipped them out in barrels for a tenth of their value or less, and made distant merchants in St. John's and England wealthy on the trade.

The salmon-catchers found great forests growing on this shore — timber trees and masts for ships — and fast rivers that would turn great water wheels for lumbering. And in the forest, too, they found both game and fur, meat for their tables, and pelts for ladies of fashion — furs for which, like the fish, they received a small fraction of their value. They were illiterate people, mostly, taking what they could get from the virgin wealth of land and sea, using only a little, and passing most of it on to others who had done nothing to earn such bounty. They always suspected that they were being cheated, but knew no way to prove it, or what to do about it if they could.

Despite such exploitation, they lived well. They needed little cash income, for mostly they lived directly on the wealth of land and sea — wealth that ranged from seals to sperm whales, from caplin to the lordly salmon, and from dovekies to migrating flocks of geese.

Then came the hard times, when the trickle of cash dried up, and men lived poor and children went naked. Then the war, when men went off to fight or to work in logging camps or to labour for fabulous wages at the building of great airports and naval docks. Then Confederation with Canada, and a government that promised pensions and wages instead of fish.

* * *

Suddenly, in April 1949, every old person was getting at least a dollar a day. A mother with half a dozen children automatically got around forty dollars a month. It seems like very little, now. But in the 1940s, to families whose average income had been $300 a year, it seemed like a fortune.

Before Confederation life for most Newfoundlanders had been an endless struggle with no prospect of any real comfort, no hope of accumulating property or putting anything aside for old age. A few lucky ones managed, through great sacrifices, to accumulate a savings account of a hundred dollars or so to buy themselves a decent funeral after they died.

The effects came more slowly to the Great Northern Peninsula than to most of Newfoundland. People with money for the first time immediately began demanding that stores stock something more than bare essentials, but the Peninsula was still isolated, and not until the road to St. Anthony was built (completed in the 1960s) did the twentieth century descend on these people like a bolt from heaven.

Then youngsters who had picked their way barefoot along cliff paths from one settlement to the next went hot-rodding from place to place at eighty miles an hour. There was no transition to the Pepsi generation. One morning, it was simply there.

This place on the edge of the world, where habitation shelves off toward the Arctic, seemed to catch always the worst of what was going on outside.

* * *

The music of mouth organs and ancient fiddles gave way to canned country and western and to bush-league hit parade. The old square dances and step dances that had been brought from Europe hundreds of years before at last went under, submerged by a curious anachronism — the American jive of the 1940s.

* * *

Today a road follows the coastal plain all the way north from Bonne

Bay to the local capital of St. Anthony. From Deer Lake, where the road leaves the Trans-Canada Highway, to St. Anthony, where it ends, is 172 miles, most of the route lying between the mountains and the sea. Along this road all the inhabitants of the Great Northern Peninsula's gulf shore have their homes. Some 20,000 people in more than a hundred little communities live on the Peninsula, their faces to the sea, their backs to the forest, their lives dependent upon both.

* * *

Houses are wood-frame, box-shaped, two-storey structures evolved locally to suit the climate. They are low-ceilinged, heavily-beamed, securely fastened down to withstand winds of a hundred miles an hour, and so strong that they can be levered off their foundations and floated on rafts to new homesites. Whole settlements, especially along the eastern shore, have moved in this way to the few places enjoying government services.

* * *

Most of the former outports on the eastern shore of the Great Northern Peninsula now lie empty, or almost so, inhabited by gulls and harbour seals, fireweed growing on their garden plots, and foxes coming down from the forest to forage for stranded fish and oil-killed birds along beaches where stores and stages used to stand.

But nothing has replaced the fishery along this shore. On the east coast of the Peninsula there is a little logging and sawmilling. On the west coast there is the national park, with jobs for perhaps a hundred people.

* * *

Wherever the people strive to preserve their way of life, they are ruled by the cycle of the year, by annual migrations of fish and game, by the violence of icefields and the march of the seasons. Winter is for net-mending and boat-building, for hunting "country meat" and for getting firewood. Then men with tough little horses, of a local breed able to live off the land, go to the forest to haul home load after load of dry spruce and fir and birch on the heavy wood sleds called catamarans. Others "knit twine," either repairing their fishing gear or making new nets for the following season.

You can fish about six months. In late autumn it is too stormy to risk leaving gear in the water. In winter and spring the sea is sealed under the lock and key of the arctic ice field. As soon as the ice moves off and breaks up — around the first of May if you're in luck, not till three or four weeks later, some years — lobstering begins. Next the salmon arrive, then the cod, all within a few weeks. Some men in large boats fish for halibut, shrimp and scallop, but most fish in skiffs fourteen to twenty feet long with engines of fifteen to twenty horsepower, and only for lobster, salmon and cod.

* * *

The pioneers here were entirely on their own, without official assistance or sponsorship. Here was no Red River Colony or Minnesota Settlement. It was a hard life — a life for survivors only. But as the

70

survivors remember it, the life was happy and rewarding in a way they cannot explain. They won, somehow, a quality of spiritual strength, a sense of pride in their hard-bought, meagre achievements. They did many things together — not just by families, but by whole communities, for the neighborhood was a kind of extended family, with everyone working in the common cause of community survival, and enjoying together the simple pleasures that people can create for themselves in primitive places.

* * *

The Great Northern Peninsula is still one of eastern Canada's most splendid regions, with the mountains and gorges of Gros Morne National Park in the south, fjord-like bays bisecting its hills in the north and east, but now it is no longer a land of pioneers; it is a human backwater, where men stagnate, or emigrate, or struggle against impossible odds to preserve a spirit and a way of life that belong to the past. These are people whom the world has left behind.

A few of the pioneers are still alive — men and women who moved here while the land was virgin, before machines arrived to exploit it, before there were organized villages or roads, or even a coastal steamer to connect them with the outside world. They are old now, these people, and they live mainly on memories, but their minds are rich with three-quarters of a century of change, a bracket of life that reaches from the wooden dory and the double-bitted hand axe to messages in living colour from the moon.

Harold Horwood
(from *Beyond the Road*)

Harold Horwood is a successful professional writer who was born in St. John's in 1923 and now resides in Nova Scotia. Some of his published titles are *White Eskimo, Tomorrow Will Be Sunday, Newfoundland, Beyond the Road,* and *The Foxes of Beachy Cove.* He was a member of the Confederate Party prior to the referendum of 1948, but later became a strong opponent of the Smallwood government. His writings show a strong inclination to celebrate the beauty of nature, and the values associated with rural life. He has been published in national and international magazines, and also appears in many anthologies.

Questions

1. The author is much more than a writer of tourist literature. Find examples of writing which support this statement.

2. The selection is excerpted from three different chapters of the book. Can you identify the author's point of view in relation to the history of the area, to the people, and the natural environment?

3. Many things which are ordinarily assumed to be improvements and signs of progress, are seen by some to be just the opposite. Can you find some examples of this in the selection? Where you can, give reasons for considering the events or changes improvements, and then give reasons for considering them the opposite.

4. What is Horwood's position relative to the policy of centralization?

Activities

1. Make a photographic essay on the communities of the east side of the Great Northern Peninsula.

2. Sketch the scene suggested in the second paragraph.

3. Write a character sketch of one of the pioneers in this part of the province.

4. Discuss formally Horwood's suggestion that the settlers did not profit from their work in fishing and furring; that they were exploited.

5. Find points of similarity between this essay and the song by P.A. Byrne entitled "West Moon".

One attraction of this short story is Helen Porter's ability to mould her concise and descriptive narration of an extended family's last days in its homeland into a memorable reminder of how closely tied Newfoundlanders are to their roots. The simplicity and depth of those roots are etched in ordinary images: boats, berries, grass, gardens, graves. The land and the sea dominate in the imagery. There are none of the sophisticated themes which characterize today's Newfoundland computer-technology society. Still, the story should not be dismissed as simplistic. The sustained irony and the emphasie placed on family roots make the story something more than itself, a significant reminder that we all should have moving days in our lives, days when we re-evaluate the important goals and purposes in life, days when we, perhaps tearfully like Jenny's mother, reject the old to get on with the new.

Moving Day

I suppose it shouldn't have come as such a shock to me really. I mean, all I heard at the University for the whole year was centralization, resettlement, relocation — the professors had a real field day, especially the ones in the Sociology Department. And the newspapers, too, it was a godsend for them. As for the politicians — well. In fact the only people who haven't had too much to say about it are the ones who are really involved in the thing. But anyway, as I said, I shouldn't have been so surprised when I heard that everybody from Grassy Island was going to move to Carlisle. It was Karen who brought it up.

"But why didn't Mom and Dad tell me?" I was talking to myself although Karen was sitting right next to me on the train.

"They probably wanted to surprise you with the good news when you got home." Karen is from Carlisle herself and of course she thinks there's no place like it.

"I can think of more pleasant surprises," I told her, and then I changed the subject. Somehow I didn't want to discuss it with Karen.

When I got home, though, I lost no time in bringing up the matter, I can tell you. They were all on the wharf to meet the boat, all except Mom and Nan, that is. It took the two of them to look after the big Welcome Home Dinner. I couldn't get a word in edgeways going up the hill, what with Cavell and Charlie asking a thousand questions. Dad didn't say much. He never does.

But when we were all sitting around the table, after Mom had hugged me and Nan had cried her little cry I let go.

"What's all this I hear about leaving Grassy Island, Mom?" It was a long time since I'd had chicken and salt meat on the same plate but I wasn't as hungry as I'd expected to be. "It's not true, I hope."

You know how they always used to say in old-fashioned books "Her face fell"? Well, that's what happened to Mom's face then. "Yes, it is true, Jenny," she said slowly. "I thought you'd be glad."

Well, after that everyone got into the act — Nan telling Mom that "everybody is not in such a rush to get away as you is, Martha," and Cavell and Charlie both saying they didn't know what anyone could see in a place like Carlisle. Even Dad had his say. "It's the women that's doing it," he told me. "If it was left to us men we'd all be content to live out our lives here."

And didn't Mom go for him when he said that — all about the men being away in the lumber woods or on the Labrador when things were really rough on the Island, and how she was sick and tired of not being able to get a doctor when she needed one, and of having her children go to a one-room school under teachers too young or too stupid to get a job anywhere else. Then when Nan said she didn't see how Mom could go away and leave the place where dear little Tommy was buried — well, that was too much even for Mom. Tommy was my little brother, died when he was three years old, pneumonia, I think it was. But Dad took up for Mom then and reminded Nan that if she was the good Christian woman she was supposed to be she'd know it wouldn't matter where the poor little body lay. The next thing I knew I was up in my room bawling my eyes out. It wasn't a bit like the kind of homecoming I'd been looking forward to for months.

I suppose I must have fallen asleep, for the next thing I knew the house was quiet and Mom was standing in the doorway just looking at me. When she saw that I was awake she came in and sat on the bed, not even pushing back the spotless white spread she always ironed so carefully.

"Try to see it my way, Jenny," she pleaded, and it did seem strange to hear Mom plead. She was usually so sure of herself.

"I'm sorry, Mom, I shouldn't have been so upset, but I can't imagine any home except this one, and I don't know how I can live if I don't have this place to come back to."

"To come back to. That's just the point, Jenny." Mom stood up then, and walked over to the window. I couldn't see her face. "I wouldn't mind coming back here for the rest of my life. But it's *living* here, day in, day out, season in, season out, year in, year out, that I can't take any longer. It was bad enough when there were twenty or more families here, but now there's only eight left, and more going all the time. Things'll get worse instead of better." She ran her hand along the shiny-painted windowsill. "If you had to settle down here yourself, Jenny, you'd know what I mean."

She did have something there, though I wasn't willing to concede it then. I had never considered settling down on Grassy Island myself, but I'm going to be a teacher, after all, so I'll *have* to go away. And then, when I do marry Ralph, he'll probably still be working in Corner Brook, where he is now, so I'll have to live there. But I had always counted on Grassy Island as being *there* when I needed it. I would never be able to feel the same way about Carlisle.

Well, somehow things got back to normal after that first awful day. It was as if we had all made up our minds, on our own, not to bring the matter up. Everything was finalized, anyhow, so what was the use? Evidently Mom had been one of the instigators of the whole project and this was what was annoying Nan. But Nan didn't have much left to say, except a scattered word under her breath and Mom ignored that.

We had a wonderful summer. Even the weather cooperated, for once, and we spent more time outdoors than in. Between the boats and the berries, the grass and the gardens, we didn't have an idle minute. It was like we couldn't get enough of it all. But you know, even though Mom didn't say another word to me about moving, except what she had to in the way of preparation, sometimes I couldn't help seeing her side of it. I still couldn't picture myself in Carlisle, but after all, I wouldn't be there very much, and it *would* be better for Mom. I had never really realized before how much she must have hated the isolation of the island all those years. It would probably turn out to be good for Cavell and Charlie, too. As for Dad, well, he seemed closer to being reconciled than he had been at first. One night I even caught him looking at the pictures of modern kitchens in Eaton's catalogue. He always did like carpentry work next best to fishing.

Mom was quieter than I ever remembered her. Sometimes I'd catch her looking at me, as if she was about to say something and then she'd change her mind. She had a lot of work to do, of course, and although Cavell and I helped she had her own way of doing things and didn't want to be interfered with too much. One night, when she was taking a batch of bread out of the oven of the old coal stove, Dad laughed and said to her, "I suppose the bread'll taste better when we gets electricity, Martha" and she snapped right back "Are you trying to tell me I don't make good bread, Peter Mead?" But most of the time she was unusually silent. I figured it was because she had her sights set on Carlisle and was almost afraid to breathe for fear something would go wrong with the plan.

But nothing did, and almost before we could turn around it was moving day. We were all standing on the wharf watching Dad load our gear aboard Uncle Job's boat. Some of it had gone on ahead of us, but there were certain things that we wouldn't take until the last day.

Cavell and Charlie were horsing around threatening to throw each other overboard, and Nan was sitting on an overturned barrel, her ankles tightly crossed, looking almost as if she was enjoying the excitement.

"Where's your mother?" she asked suddenly. "I thought by the way she been dyin' to get out of here that she'd be the first one on board."

"She must have gone back to the house for something. Run up and get her, Jenny, we're almost ready," Dad said, and I was off like a flash.

Mom was just standing in the middle of the kitchen when I got there and I had the "Hurry up" formed on my lips before I got a good look at her. Even though her back was towards me the sight of her shoulders was enough to make me swallow the words I was about to say. Quiet though she was, I knew that she was sobbing her heart out.

I slipped out of the house and hurried back to the wharf. I felt I shouldn't hang around. "Mom'll be down in a minute," I told Dad. "She's just...having a last look."

I wondered if I should tell him more but just at that moment his eyes met mine and I could see there was no need. "I'll go and get her myself, Jenny maid," he said, and our eyes followed him as he ran up the path. Even Nan didn't have a word to say.

Helen Porter

Helen Porter is from St. John's, the old North American seaport about which she has written extensively and passionately. Frequently anthologized, her poems and stories have been featured in CBC productions and in such periodicals as *Chatelaine*, *Star Weekly*, and *Weekend*. She has frequently taken time to visit schools and to evaluate student writings. Her major published work is *Below the Bridge*, an autobiographical account of growing up on the St. John's Southside.

Questions

1. Why is it ironic that Jenny has most to say about the splendour of outport living?

2. Using quotations from the story along with your own words, briefly describe what each character will miss at Carlisle.

3. What symbolism do you find in the first three lines of the name of the place to which the Grassy Islanders will shift?

4. At the end of the story who was sobbing most? Why?

5. What problems will the Grassy Islanders face at Carlisle? Select statements from the story that suggest the nature of these problems. Will they solve these problems? Explain why you think they will or will not.

Activities

1. Write a script and act out the following scenes:

   a. Jenny talks to Karen on the train.
   b. The family greets Jenny at the wharf.
   c. Mom is in Jenny's bedroom when Jenny awakes.
   d. Jenny is picking bakeapples and talking to herself aloud.
   e. Mom is in her kitchen, crying.

2. Turn this short story into one or more ballads and use your verses to make a class singalong.

3. Imagine you are camping in the Terra Nova National Park and keeping a diary. Write out the entries for several days during which you met people from the surrounding

communities whose populations have swollen because of resettlement from the Bonavista Bay Islands in the area. (Glovertown would be a good representative town.) Record your thoughts and feelings after you have listened to one who had to leave his place of birth after having spent over fifty years there fishing; one who had lost her infant son there while stormbound in a winter blizzard; one who wanted to watch wrestling on TV but had no electricity; one who wanted to take chemistry but had no high school teacher; one who had helped build a new stage and slipway the year before everyone left; one who had shifted at his own expense and scorned others who had shifted at Government expense; one whose husband and three children (the entire family besides herself) are buried on the island of her birth; one whose only income was for janitorial services performed at the little schoolhouse on the hill.

4. Write a series of letters inviting persons with firsthand resettling experience to your class. Follow up with thank you notes after the visits.

5. Research the following topics, using the short story as your springboard into sociology and history:

a. History of and attitudes towards Centralization as a Newfoundland Government program. (Examine attitudes objectively *before* you judge the program's success or failure.)
b. History of and attitudes toward Resettlement as a Newfoundland phenomenon.
c. Contributions of Centralization to community growth in Newfoundland.
d. Resettlement before Confederation versus Resettlement after Confederation.
e. The etymology of some the terms used in the Centralization program.
f. The famous Centralization court case at Glovertown.
g. Prepare a list of the names of Newfoundland settlements which today are populated, largely, by resettled people. Find out the contribution of these resettled folks to their new

community. (Hint: Well prepared interview sheets administered to all willing people will make your work more efficient.)

h. Prepare a list of abandoned Newfoundland outports.

In "Leave-Taking" Geraldine Rubia catches some of the main characteristics of both man and woman in Newfoundland — independence, ruggedness, and passion — by presenting two vivid literary vignettes each of which is both lyrical and dramatic. The sense of place is strong in Rubia's poem, although there are no references to specific places and persons. Instead the general spirit of the people abandoning their outport homes and the remote seaside is raised to a universal level, people's relationship with their homelands being an ancient and universal theme. Extremely terse and emotionally gripping rather than philosophical, this poem does not attempt to express any verdict on Newfoundland resettlement. (In this respect it is like Tom Dawe's "Abandoned Outport".) It does, however, reverse the norm: typically, the women wished to leave the outports for educational, medical, shopping, and entertainment reasons; typically, the men wished to stay for employment reasons; in Rubia's poem, the old woman will not go and the old fisherman dreams of leaving his nets so he can paint his new dwelling and yarn with his new neighbours. This surprise element adds a fresh touch to an old theme, and it is reinforced by the poetic techniques of dialogue, cadence and stress, repetition, the use of words that appeal to the senses — particularly to the senses of hearing and seeing, and an impressionistic style disguised as a dramatic style.

Leave-Taking

The Old Woman

Rock-forbidden roses on her walls
gleaming kettle coming to a boil
no neighbors any more for tea
who needed them
her home was all.
Thin driftwood brittle fingers
clutching at her door
she faces her husband
on the rain-bright pebble path

    "I'm not going, I tell you.
    What's there for me?"
    (Old devil, he
    always was the one
    to gad about)

The Old Fisherman

Bone-forbidden sea behind his back
no nets to mend
no boat to haul up on the rocks
another dwelling waiting for his touch
paint peeling fence falling
naked for a porch,
neighbors there
to yarn with on the wharf.
He pries the clinging fingers loose

"Come on now mother,
you'll love it, wait and see."
(Stubborn old woman, she
always was the one
to make a fuss)

Geraldine Rubia

A biographical note on the author appears on page 12.

Questions

1. What is the dominant impression of the outport home created by the poet in vignette one?

2. How do the following words or phrases in the first vignette contribute to this dominant impression: "roses", "kettle", "no neighbours", "who needed them"? Are there unexpected elements here?

3. Comment on the suitability of the words "behind", "no nets", "no boats", in the second vignette. Afterwards comment on the suitability of "another dwelling", "naked", "yarn". Would you say the old fisherman is a lover of life?

4. Do you think the husband expects his wife to remain behind long? Explain.

5. The old woman is a stubborn attention seeker. The old man is a happy-go-lucky jack-of-all-trades. Comment.

Activities

1. Sketch in pencil a leave-taking scene in which the old woman with "driftwood brittle fingers" clutches her door while her

husband tries to pry her loose. If time permits, turn your sketch into a work of art using paints or clay or some other artistic tools/materials.

2. Find and visit a person who had firsthand experience with the kind of leave-taking described in the poem. What are your impressions now that you have two views of the same event?

Like the seventeenth-century poet Andrew Marvell who could at his
back "...always hear/Time's winged chariot hurrying near," the
twentieth-century Al Pittman recalls nostalgically the time when St.
Leonard's used to enjoy its "green and salty days." In the first stanza
the poet and his friends are sad and happy about time. The wildflowers
growing on the hillside beside the sea and the tides changing with
the hours make the present joyful for them. Yet at the same time the
image of death — "cremated foundations of long-ago homes" —
makes them sad. Perhaps the most memorable treatment of the twin
themes of time and death is found in the second stanza in which even
the holy church has succumbed and become merely a holding ground
for rocks and roses. In the last stanza the reader is presented with a
striking contrast, that between the haunting experience of the poet and
his friends reflecting sadly on the effect of time and decay on the outport,
and the ordinary experience of the men offshore fishing who are unaware
of what time and death have done to the people and community of
St. Leonard's.

St. Leonard's Revisited

We came ashore
where wildflower hills
tilted to the tide
and walked
sad and gay
among the turnip cellars
tripping over the cremated
foundations
of long-ago homes
half-buried
in the long years' grass

almost reverently
we walked among the rocks
of the holy church
and worshipped roses
in the dead yard
and came again to the cove
as they did after rosary
in the green and salty days

and men offshore
hauling traps
wondered what ghosts
we were

walking with the forgotten sheep
over the foothigh grass paths
that led
like trapdoors
to a past
they could hardly recall

Al Pittman

Mr. Pittman was born in St. Leonard's, Placentia Bay, a community which has been resettled. He presently is a member of the English Department of Sir Wilfred Grenfell College in Corner Brook. His writings have been widely anthologized, including poems, short stories, essays and plays. Among his published works are *The Elusive Resurrection, Seaweed and Rosaries, Through One More Window, Once When I Was Drowning, A Rope Against The Sun, Down By Jim Long's Stage,* and *A Wonderful Fine Day for a Sculpin Named Sam.* His drama has been produced by CBC Radio, and performed on stage across Canada. Mr. Pittman has also been in demand as a reader sponsored by The Canada Council, and the National Book Festival. During a period when he lived in Tobago he completed work on *West Moon,* a major play to be published in the near future.

Questions

1. What is the theme of the poem?

2. Abandoned villages are symbols of eternal sadness and at the same time symbols of joyful memories. How is this statement true of the poem?

3. How is the death of an outport a spiritual as well as a physical event?

4. What is your interpretation of "tilted to the tide", "long years' grass", "worshipped roses", "the green and salty days", "like trapdoors"?

5. How are the last two lines appropriate for the poem's ending?

Activities

1. Draw a map of Newfoundland and write in the locations of towns which have been abandoned. Try to find a brief history of some of them, especially those which might be near where you live.

2. Read the poem aloud. Choose suitable music for background. Try different approaches until you feel that you have captured the mood which you think best suits the poem.

3. Read other poems about time and death. Some examples are Dylan Thomas's "Fern Hill", Phillip Larkin's "Lines on a Young Lady's Photograph Album", and John Crowe Ransom's "Blue Girls". Compare and contrast the treatment of time and death in these poems with that in "St. Leonard's Revisted". Present your work orally to your class.

4. Sketch some of the scenes suggested by the poem.

West Moon Song

1. Oh, tonight the west moon hangs over the harbour,
   Shines down 'cross the headland and out 'cross the bay,
   Shines down through the trees and rests on the graveyard,
   The only reminder of a long ago day.

2. But my mind takes me back to a time in that harbour,
   When stout boats at anchor dozed on the sway,
   When the laughter of children sent glad cries to heaven,
   And women looked seaward from meadows of hay.

3. But no longer I see those fish-covered flakes now,
   No green rows of garden stretched over the hill,
   No punt in the beach gleaming red with fresh copper,
   No fine sturdy stick freshly cut for a keel.

4. For the government men came bribing and preaching,
   They convinced all the livyers to just move away,
   Now they're scattered like dry leaves from hell to high water,
   But the wind and the west moon elected to stay.

5. So tonight the west moon hangs over the harbour,
   Shines down 'cross the headland and out 'cross the bay,
   Shines down through the trees and rests on the graveyard,
   As if looking for the souls of the ones moved away.

Pat Byrne

West Moon

Oh, to-night the West Moon hangs o-ver the har-bour——, shines
down cross the head-land and out cross the bay——, shines
down thro' the trees and rests on the grave-yard——, the
on-ly re-mind-er of a long-a-go day.

V. 2.

My mind takes me back to a time in that har-bour——, when
stout boats at an-chor dozed on the sway——, when the
laugh-ter of child-ren sent glad cries to Heav-en——, and
wo-men looked sea-ward from mead-ows of hay.

V. 3 lines 2 + 3

no green rows of gar-den stretched ov-er the hill——, no
punt in the beach gleaming red with fresh cop-per,

Arrangement by Sheila Brown

UNIT 3

Introspection

Introspection

Few people are so certain of their place in life, so sure of their understanding of their surroundings or so confident in their beliefs or philosophies, that they have no inclination to pose questions for themselves. It seems that poets in particular tend to question aspects of their lives, and of the world in which they live, or to express wonder and admiration of things which others take for granted. This unit presents poems which are examples of the positing of such questions and concerns as themes. An examination is offered of violence and gentleness as parts of nature, and their extension into human nature is questioned. We ask if the past is really past when we can be heated by the sunshine of a hundred or more years ago. Does farming in poor soil produce more for us than just crops? Is there meaning to beauty or bravery when it is not observed or known? Fatalism is examined — are events inevitable? Seldom do the poets give answers or conclusions, but they always throw new light on the topic; we see and think differently after the encounter with the poem. And that is what the authors intend. This is a unit to be enjoyed intellectually as well as aesthetically. There should be ample time for discussion, but we should realize that there are seldom single correct responses or conclusions.

This poem presents a social-psychological statement, and asks a philosophical question. The author uses a clear concrete example as the vehicle, and enhances the intellectual stimulation by using exceptionally appropriate metaphors.

This Morning I Sat

This morning I sat
indolent and limp
against a window pane
and watched a frantic sparrow
defying my lean cat.

The cat was taut
with leap and speed
and stealth and strength.
The bird had only poetry to wield
and lost.

Cats eat up grace with relish.
But they are poets too
and can create cunning
and flights of terror
with their eyes.

A small shudder
rippled down my flesh.

Do I have wings or claws?

Rosalie Fowler

Rosalie Fowler was born in St. John's and now lives in Corner Brook. Her published poems indicate a fine ability to use poetic devices to present her thoughts with precision.

Questions

1. Is the question posed a universal one? Explain.

2. What do you understand by:

   a. "The bird had only poetry to wield and lost."

   b. "Cats eat up grace with relish."?

Activities

1. Why would the author be sitting "indolent and limp against a window pane."

2. Discuss the application of the thought of the poem to some social situation.

3. Sketch the scene presented in the poem.

4. Read "Train Window" by Robert Finch. Compare the precision of the two poems.

5. Read "The Tyger" by William Blake. Compare the themes of the two poems.

Mr. Elliot speculates on the thoughts and motives of Thomas, one of the Apostles, also called Didymus, on the day after Jesus was crucified. Little is known of Thomas, other than that he was of a doubting nature, and that he was brave. Here he analyzes what has happened, why he has believed in Jesus, and what he should do next. We know, of course, that the story is not finished, and that he will meet the risen Jesus, and that the pessimism of the last line will be erased. The reference to Judah can be checked in the fifteenth chapter of the Book of Joshua. The slaying of the children is found in the Gospel of Matthew, Chapter Two, and the killing of the king of the Amalekites is described in First Samuel, Chapter Fifteen, verse thirty-three. It might be best if a reading of Chapter eighteen to twenty-one of the Gospel According to Saint John preceded the reading of the poem.

Didymus on Saturday

I who have trusted only certainties,

Save for a three-years dream, awake at last.

Now Jesus has his grave, Judas his gold,

Peter his praise, he of the ready sword.

I, who believed in all my disbelief,

Am left with nothing but the biting shame

That gnaws me for believing easily.

It seemed at times a thing beyond mere proof

That he was king of Judah, son of God.

His crown was made of thorns and he was nailed

Fast to a narrow cross with Roman spikes.

I saw him walk to death between two thieves,

A little man whose face was cracked with fear

And a tall man whose eyes were dull with doom.

The flesh was fixed to the complacent wood,

The crosses lifted up and downward flung,

Jolting into the jarring earth-sockets.

A triple scream splintered the quiet dawn,

And death could overtake them at his leisure,

Being so fastened.

The mob shrilled with delight to see such pain,
And that was yesterday and he is dead.
My world was ended with a hammer stroke.
I might have known, I might have known, I might have known:
He was too just to be a king of Judah,
He was too kind to be a son of God
Who slew the children by the muddy Nile
And had the king of the Amalekites
Cloven to pieces in the sacred shambles.
Yet, hard is the awakening from my dream,
I must take care to guard against more dreams.
Some say that he will rise and from his grave
Spring like a sleeper from a restful bed
To justify his godhead. Not for me
Subscription to these fancies. Not if he
Spoke to me in the voice that tuned my heart
To think him God; not if he broke the bread
Of love at my own table; not if he
Were seen by John, who cannot tell a lie.
And all proofs tangible and ocular
Will not convince me save I touch the wound
The Roman spear made in his dying side,
Press the torn palms, embrace the stricken feet.

Tomorrow is the first day of the week
And I shall leave this gray Jerusalem
Where he lies sleeping in the hollowed stone,
Never to come into his kingdom now.

David Elliott
(from *A Suite for Easter*)

David Elliot was born in eastern Newfoundland. He presently lives in Corner Brook where he has been a member of the English faculty of Sir Wilfred Grenfell College.

Questions

1. Thomas says he has "trusted only certainties, /Save for a three year's dream...." What does he mean? Why are these the first lines of the poem?

2. Thomas is questioning a number of things in the poem. Can you put three of them into your own words and suggest their importance to the overall structure of the poem?

3. What is the effect of the repetition of "I might have known..."? How should that line be read?

4. How can you explain Thomas's intention to "take care to guard against more dreams."?

Activities

1. Write a character sketch of Thomas as Elliot portrays him.

2. Explain:
   a. "I, who believed in all my disbelief..."
   b. "It seemed at times a thing beyond mere proof..."
   c. "...too just to be a king of Judah, he was too kind to be a son of God..."
   d. "Never to come into his kingdom now."

3. Listen to Mr. Elliot read his poem on the Pigeon Inlet recording "Ten Newfoundland Poets". Read the poem aloud yourself.

4. Read "The Death of Samson" by John Milton. Compare the style with this poem.

5. Read "The Journey of the Magi" by T.S. Eliot. Compare the techniques with those in this poem.

In this sonnet our attention is drawn to the age old question of the nature of reality. Does a sound not heard by any ear actually exist? The poet asks the question about the beauty of trees unseen in the deep forest, and he answers it positively, for they exist in the eye of God. The poem has a simple rhyme scheme made up of rhyming couplets, however it is unusual in the lack of end-stopped lines and the use of hysteron proterons. The style is traditional and the diction poetic but simple. The theme is a different version of "the heavens declare the glory of God."

Silver Birches

I like to watch the great trees in our park;

To take their shade in sunshine, and nigh dark

To listen to the rustling of the wind

Amongst their leaves, but it is sweet to find,

Here in this wilderness, with no path nigh,

These birches, that by chance engaged mine eye

From yonder hill. How admirable, trees,

That take no thought at all of praise, for these

Have few to look upon them; none the less,

Do they, though cloistered in this wilderness,

The glory of their God confess, and shine

As worshippers, that haply here divine

Their purpose high, for trees remote, like these,

Can rarely have more than their God to please.

R. A. Parsons

Richard Augustus Parsons was born in Bay Roberts, Conception Bay, and practiced law in St. John's for most of his adult life. His poetry reflects a keen eye for the beauties of nature, and a firm belief in God's love for his creations. Mr. Parsons has been honored by various institutions, including Memorial University. He died in St. John's in 1982.

Questions

1. What are the practical uses of trees from Mr. Parson's perspective? Why does he mention this at the beginning?

2. How does Mr. Parsons indicate that the spiritual use of trees is more important than any other?

Activities

1. State the contention of the octave. Reword the conclusion of the sestet.

2. Sketch a scene which might represent the poem.

3. Give examples from the poem which illustrate the traditional style.

The sardonic mood of this poem is used to convey the poet's ambivalence in relation to Newfoundland's position within Canadian society, and the undefinable yet enduring attraction which the province has for those who live here. The reference to Royal Commissions and Wheat Boards underlines this. His solution to the problem posed is not unfamiliar to us, since his intention is to obtain a federal grant to fund it as a study.

Essence of Wild Newfunlan

I am looking for my essence,

    (What makes us always want to stay here, anyway?)

Give me ways —

  1. Fire me from my job at the oil refinery.

      Repossess my new skidoo.

      Raise the price of everything again!

          Then take me, naked, to the Buchans Barrens and

              leave me there.

          (in warm weather, with no flies)

      Will I struggle back,

      birch boughs covering my privates,

      to get a good meal of fish and brewis?

      Or will I grow moose hair and antlers

      and get myself killed

      by mainland hunters?

      It's open to discussion.

      Set up a Royal Commission to inquire into it.

  II. Perhaps a more scientific method would be

          to let me stay

          and pay me $25,000 a year

          to organize a Newfoundland branch of the

              Wheat Board.

      Put a ban on rabbit catching and birding,

      Make me take up the few lobster pots I put in the

          water,

And let me pick berries only in designated areas.

Would I still be happy? Would money alone satisfy
me?

What about the control group?

III   Stop! I have it!

Shut off all car ferries to North Sydney.

Transplant 100,000 people from Mississauga

    (in each community according to population)

and follow up with these in two years —

    The accent variance test B

    folklore recall (schedule 419)

    productivity-dole ratio.

Ah me b'ys, I think I have found a way!

    (with the aid of Federal money)

Kevin Major

Kevin Major was born in Stephenville in western
Newfoundland. He has completed university degrees in
science and education. His teaching brought him into daily
contact with young people and it was largely this which
encouraged him to write his first novel, *Holdfast*. He has
won numerous awards for his writing for young adults, but
is not as well known for his poetry. The poem illustrates
Major's ability to control shape and structure precisely in
making a subtle and not easily conveyed point. Mr. Major
lives on the Eastport Peninsula with his wife and son. His
second novel, *Far From Shore*, was published in 1980, and
a third, *Thirty-Six Exposures*, in 1984.

Questions

1. Which of the three divisions of the poem is most heavily satiric?

2. Are there suggestions in the poem that some government
   people do not understand Newfoundland? List them.

3. What is the significance of the spelling in the title?

4. In addition to opening the poem, what function does the first
   line serve?

Activities

1. Discuss with others what it is that makes Newfoundland a unique part of the Canadian Confederation.

2. Find more information about:
   a. "...the oil refinery."
   b. "...the Buchans Barrens..."
   c. "...the Wheat Board."
   d. "...the people from Mississauga..."

3. Read "The Provinces" by A.M. Klein. Make a comment relating the two poems.

4. Read "A Modest Proposal" by Jonathan Swift. Compare the suggestions of the two works from the point of view of the author's intention in proposing it.

*The poem is an address to all the men who manned the "fish-boxes"
and other schooners sailing in and from Newfoundland. The poet
celebrates the heroic and epic deeds of schoonermen as they faced the
storms and challenges of the ocean, and the vagaries of weather and
coastline. The pleasant times are remembered too, the nights of clear
starlight, and the calms which gave time for relaxation and reverie.
The poem has a simple rhyme scheme, and is constructed of Spencerian
stanzas. The poet's ability to represent sights, sounds and action is
well demonstrated.*

Schoonerman

Come! Schoonerman, we'll talk of stormy weather;
Of cold seas, and the lore of little ships;
Of lines and twines, and ways with wood and leather
This land has bred into your fingertips.
We'll work the wind and tide without misgiving;
We'll ride the dories over and away,
And listen to the seabird's wild thanksgiving
Above the trap-berth at the break of day.

Remember, when you hauled the icy buoyline,
A fresh nor'wester blowing full to sea;
The snow-capped headlands gnawing at the skyline;
A thousand leagues of ocean on your lee.
You sensed the hungry chasms down below you;
The glowering wind-blown heavens overhead;
The reefs that seemed to watch, and wait, and know you.
And yet, you felt no twinge of doubt or dread.

Remember, when the day and toil was ended,
You sat on deck, and pondered moon and star,
And heard, away, where light and shadow blended,
The mad Atlantic slumbering on the bar.
While moonlight charmed the dull face of existence,
And west winds spoke in their enchanted tongue,
You felt that spell of mystery and distance,
That drew men to the sea since time was young.

Remember, when the rain-splashed skylight glistened
Against the reeky blackness all around,
That, to you, ever crept, and paused, and listened
Until it seemed to smother every sound.
Save, now and then, the fretful, restless creaking
Of the mainmast as it argued with the shrouds,
Or when, again, like startled demons shrieking,
A siren's blast came tearing through the clouds.

Remember, yet the midnight and the thunder;
The hissing, rearing, avalanching seas;
The mighty gust that ripped the sails asunder;
The awful plunge that flung you to your knees.
There, at your post, upon the sea-swept quarter,
Half blinded by the sting of driving hail,
And battered by the rush of frenzied water,
You fought another battle with the gale.

Gregory Power

Mr. Power was born in Dunville, Placentia Bay, and has lived most of his adult life in St. John's. He was active in politics, serving for several years in the cabinet of Premier Smallwood. He was an outstanding athlete in his early years, and won major awards. He has also received recognition as a writer, especially for his poetry and satire.

Questions

1. What reasons are there for the celebration of the schoonerman in Newfoundland?

2. Which of the dangers mentioned seems most ominous? Why?

3. While the schoonerman engaged in physical battle with the elements what would his wife or mother be doing? Which situation would be hardest to endure? Why?

Activities

1. Scan the first stanza to determine the rhythm. Would a

different metre improve the poem? Discuss how the rhythm is important to the content.

2. Read "Newfoundland" by E.J. Pratt. Connect the two poems thematically.

3. Sketch a schooner. If you don't know the details examine the picture of "The Luetta" on page fifty-four of *The Newfoundland Fish Boxes* by Dr. Harry D. Roberts. (Brunswick Press, Fredericton, 1982).

4. Read of Captain Bob Bartlett's experiences as a schoonerman in *The Log of Bob Bartlett*, G.P. Putnam's Sons, New York, 1928.

5. Read Barbour's *Forty-Eight Days Adrift*, Breakwater, St. John's, 1982.

This is an elegy in the traditional mode. The language is elevated, and the emotion on a grand scale. The poet uses intense personification in the opening lines, and follows with comparisons which place his hero properly with the great heroes of Polar exploration. Metaphors carry the poem to its conclusion. The separation into two uneven sections, each with its separate purpose, suggest a sonnet form, but the poem is not a true sonnet. Notice the poet's use of the dash, perhaps in an attempt to intensify emotion.

Varick Frissell

(Died in *Viking* disaster at Icefields, 1931)

She has taken him to her jealous breast —
The great white mother of the northern night;
And wound her snowy hair around him — tight,
To place him starry-eyed among the rest
Of that white company, whom her frozen might
Have conquered: Franklin, Scott, Amundsen, bright
And gallant comrades for the last long quest.

And we have lost him — O God, it seems
That we must ever lose the young and brave;
That they march forward to an unmarked grave
Too soon, and leave us broken hearts and dreams.
Yet through the choking tears we smile and save
The dream — the star that through the dark night gleams.

Irving Fogwill

Irving Fogwill was born in St. John's in 1901. He was active in politics as a Confederate at the time of the National Convention. His writing has been published in two volumes, *Prelude to Doom*, and *A Short Distance Only*. He died in 1984 in St. John's.

Questions

1. Who were Franklin, Scott and Amundsen? Varick Frissell was a movie director who died in the *Viking* explosion in 1931 while completing work on the movie "The Viking". What is your opinion of the poet's placing him in company with the others?

2. What words and phrases in the poem could be used to illustrate the elevated style?

3. Why does the poet choose to make the "great white mother of the northern night" seem to be the cause of Frissell's death, when the actual cause was an explosion of unknown origin?

Activities

1. Obtain and view the film "The Viking" which was completed by Frissell in 1930. His trip in 1931 was to obtain exciting footage to make the film a little more commercially viable.

2. Read about Frissell in Chapter eight of *Sails Over Ice* by Captain Bob Bartlett. (Charles Scribner's Sons, New York, 1934). Bartlett was the captain of the *Viking* in 1930, and also an actor in the film.

3. Read "Break, Break, Break" or "The Splendour Falls" by Lord Tennyson. Compare either with this poem as an elegy, or poem about death.

The poet comments on this poem: "It is about a boy who is riding his bike away from school for the summer holidays. It says something about Pascal's fear of randomness. It might be, for someone else, about predestination. In any event the poem creates, and generates, its own myth." The reader should pay particular attention to the speed and exhuberance of the young rider as he leaves the humdrum to meet the intersection of two shadows. The poet's use of metaphor ("blunted arrows of daydreams") and similes ("books/obscure as oceans;") makes the boy, his motives and his actions particularly vivid.

Shadows: Jamie's Last Ride

His life is prologue
He is centaur, flesh
welded to steel;
he leans
to the spinning stirrups

His mind
(brimming with summer)

outraces him;
like the oblique shadow
skimming the ditch, it is always
ahead

He is leaving behind
the soulless rooms
pedestrian teachers,
books
obscure as oceans;
he is leaving behind
the blunted arrows of daydreams

He has no thought or time
for the car (the other mind)
or Pascal's geometry:
two inexorable lines
surging
to intersect

The shadows merge
explode

It still unfolds, still rushes
back to nowhere:
   a history dreamed
   a parable of road

Enos Watts

A biographical note on the author is to be found on page 40.

Questions

1. This poem is an example of free verse. What aspects of its prosody make it so?

2. What is the purpose in referring to the car as "(the other mind)"?

3. Who was Pascal? What is the significance of the intersecting lines?

4. There is a certain objectivity in the last part of the poem which contrasts with the poet's empathizing with the boy in the earlier stanzas. Why does the poet make this change?

Activities

1. Discuss fatalism, predestination, and other beliefs which minimize man's ability to control his destiny.

2. The poet seems to appreciate what it is like to be a student finally free of school, books, and teachers. Evaluate the poet's success in this.

3. Explain:
    a. "He is centaur..."
    b. "pedestrian teachers..."
    c. "two Inexorable lines..."
    d. "a parable of road"

This poem is a sonnet, nearly Petrarchan in form (although the second quatrain does not repeat the rhyme scheme of the first.) The octave presents the picture of the men venturing onto the ocean, and the woman's fears. The sestet is separate in time and presents the result of the activity in the octave. The tragedy is suggested, rather than made explicit, which tends to make it more intense. Notice that the lines run into each other; they are not end-stopped. The poet also uses hysteron proterons ("Both backs together pull..."). *The juxtaposition of man and nature works successfully to combine main elements of the poem.*

Two Men Went Out

She watched the skimming oarblades flashing by —
Both backs together pull, they round the head —
While there she stood, lost in some nameless dread,
Until the sea recalled, with its persistent sigh,
The daily task; but even when she'd thrown
Herself with zeal into the common round
Whose was that icy hand she found
Along her back? Why seemed each noise a groan?

And late that day two pewter seagulls came:
Along the beach like two cursed souls forlorn
They flew, and screeched as if in agony;
And fishermen next day, in searching, came
Upon an old, familiar powder-horn
which bobbed beside a capsized boat at sea.

Harold Paddock

Harold Paddock is a linguist working at Memorial University. His poems are sometimes written in dialect, but more often his style is traditional. Much of his work is concerned with topics directly related to Newfoundland.

Questions

1. What are the advantages of the sonnet form in presenting the substance of this poem?

2. Is there a philosophy or belief hinted at in this poem? If so, what is it?

3. Why does the poet write "While there she stood" rather than "While she stood there"?

Activities

1. Read "The Groundswells" by E.J. Pratt. Compare the themes of the two poems.

2. Find examples of metaphor, simile, alliteration and personification in this poem.

The physical shape of the poem on the page is at once noticable. The relentlessly increasing lines have the effect of increasing intensity and energy as the reader is drawn on to the end of each of the three stanzas. Notice that the last two lines of each stanza have little punctuation to allow pausing. The first stanza is made up of one sentence, and, in effect, so are the other two. The first highlights the difficulty with soil and climate in Newfoundland, the second elaborates on the difficulty caused by a short growing season, but the third twists the thought so that disadvantages are seen as positive factors in producing a positive harvest of human qualities.

A Newfoundland Garden

Rock

and shovel

strike out sparks

that will not warm

this frozen ground until

our April showers of snow,

May gales and shivering fogs in June

are plucked away, and winter veers to scorching sun

without the grace or interception of a gentling spring.

Dig

like dogs

for spud growth

and turnip greens!

between parentheses

(Victoria to Races Day)

plant and hoe and trench, and think

to reap, as August evening coolly drawing in

before September's threat of frost, may turn our greens

to yellow limp, and rot our spuds to pulpy mushroom ooze.

God's

bitterness

upon this land?

perhaps his irony,

to let such labor bear

so little fruit, but from the toil

make bodies like our enemy the rock;

and yield a subtler harvest to our souls,

tempered in patience and low expectation that may serve

to help us endure in rougher gardens than the spud-and-turnip field.

Percy Janes

Percy Janes was born and lives in St. John's. He is best known as a writer of prose, having several novels and short stories published. He was the first recipient of the Lydia Campbell Award for writing presented by the Newfoundland and Labrador Arts Council.

Questions

1. What image of Newfoundland as a physical environment is presented in the poem? How is this used by Mr. Janes to achieve the purpose of the poem?

2. What specifics are used to make clear that the author is actually referring to Newfoundland?

Activities

1. Rearrange the lines in the stanzas so that they have a more even length. Read the poem and comment on the differences you notice.

2. Find examples of rhetorical diction, alliteration, figurative language and personification.

The essential thought of this poem is found in the last four lines. It seems like a fresh and new thought because the poet has skillfully brought us to it through the use of familiar images and actions, and intimate conversational diction. The first person plural is used to encourage our acceptance of the incidents and results by linking the speaker and the action. The setting is rural, and the life style alluded to is simple and straightforward. But we should notice that the descriptions are detailed and accurate, and sometimes the language is vivid in its imagery.

Bogwood

The year we plowed the river field, we found,
   Deep in the silt, the warped and blackened bones
Of ancient trees; and most of them were sound,
   Though every bit as heavy as the stones.
Among them there were ribs, backbones, and knees,
   Thin fingers that had held green leaves, or fed
White blossoms to the wind, lost springs, when these
   Made magic here. For days, we harvested
These bones of trees from soft, black furrows where
   The land was wet; and when the field was done
We left them in loose tangles, here and there,
   To season in the summer wind and sun.

Around the coast, old custom sets a time
   For certain work, and in our neighbourhood,
When April comes we tidy up and lime;
   December is the month for getting wood.
So, while the meadows slept, benumbed and white,
And skies were little more than half-awake,
   We cut them into junks, and they were light
As feathers now, but hard enough to break
   An axeman's heart. One bitter night we burned
This wood that time had tempered in the mire;

It charmed those hours of rest, when we concerned
Ourselves with dreams, and made a ghostly fire.
Beyond its blue, transparent flame, we saw
The heat waves dancing in a parched July;
Its light, transformed by some enchanted law,
Was hoarded sunlight from an age gone by.

Gregory Power

A biographical note on the author is to be found on page 99.

Questions

1. What indications are there in this poem that the setting is rural Newfoundland?

2. What aspects of language make this poem an exceptionally attractive one to read?

Activities

1. Express the theme of this poem as precisely as you can. Is the realization that heat from the sun of ages gone by is released to heat the poet and his family, a startling one? Can you think of other similar examples which collapse time?

2. Sketch "the blackened bones of ancient trees..."

3. Explain:

   a. "as heavy as the stones..."
   b. "...lost springs/when these made magic here..."

4. Discuss with others some possible meanings for:

   a. "Among them there were ribs, backbones and knees..."
   b. "Around the coast, old custom sets a time / For certain work..."
   c. "...when we concerned / Ourselves with dreams..."

A child's confidence in the magical, mysterious, larger-than-life actions of his grandfather is the theme of this poem. The viewpoint is that of the child, so we accept readily the unreality of the effect of the bell booming on all things in the environment. This poem is carefully crafted. Notice the use and effect of repetition, the continued insistence on "paleness" which by contrast make the grandfather stand out sharply.

Lines for My Grandfather Long Gone

I keep one memory only
of you.

I am four
and slightly shy.

You are anciently old
and brave among cows.

It is afternoon
The yard is pale in pale light.

I sit on your doorstep
waiting for anything to happen.

You unhook the gate,
stroll through it, hook
it again and stroll straight
to the old church bell hanging
heavily rusted in the corner
of the yard.

You reach out
and pull the rope.

The bell booms over the village,
booms over the sea, the hills,
the hayfields, and up into the heavens.

The yard is pale in pale light.

You stand quietly still.
Nothing moves except your arm,

your hand on the rope.

I sit on your doorstep
waiting for something to happen.

The bell booms.

You stand magically, mysteriously
still, your hand on the rope,
your pale gaze surveying the field,
the sea, the sky.

The bell booms.

In the field the cows
stop chewing. They stand
in the still hay like pathetic statues,
their tails bronzed in absurd geometry.

On the sea the perpetual waves
roll motionless in their rhythmic run
to the beach. They tilt in poised
suspension above the still suspended swell.

In the sky the frivolous birds
halt in their hurried flight. They hang
like tiny black moons stationary
and still in the pale heavens.

I sit still as stone
on your doorstep watching.

Your hand on the rope stops.

The bell stops.

The field, the sea, the sky
thrive again in a confusion of movement.

I sit on your doorstep watching.
I wonder what in the world has happened.

You come strolling down
from the corner of the yard,
the thinnest of smiles upon your mouth.

You touch your ancient hand
gently to my bewildered head.
You pass me by and go into the house,
the door closing quietly behind you.

Al Pittman

113

A biographical note on the author is to be found on page 83.

Questions

1. Why is it important that we are told early in the poem that the grandfather is "brave among cows"?

2. How does the poet convey the child's concept of the slow passage of time without actually "spelling it out" for us?

3. What is the type and form of the poem? What poetic devices make it effective?

Activities

1. Give examples of the author's use of contrast to achieve highlights.

2. Select and play music which would be appropriate to accompany a reading of this poem.

3. Define "anciently old" from the child's point of view.

4. Sketch one of the scenes in the poem.

5. Discuss the part that memory might have played in shaping the poem.

6. Read "Fern Hill" by Dylan Thomas. Compare the styles of the two poets.

7. Listen to Mr. Pittman read this poem on "Newfoundland Poets", Pigeon Inlet Productions No. 7313.

UNIT 4

Wildlife and People

Wildlife and People

An invaluable part of the environment of this province is a rich, abundant and varied wildlife. Each species, and almost every individual creature, occupies its own place in the wild, fulfilling its role as it is determined by the natural order of things. This systematic natural order and progression of birth, life, and death, of growth and decay, of prey and predator, has a beauty and serenity matched only by the fluidity of movement and perfection of form of the creatures themselves.

Whether the wildlife is that of the land, the water, or the air, it is part of the familiar environment of the people, and the response of the people to it has been expressed in many ways in our literature. The response and the point of view of the individual varies as a function of time, tradition, geography, or circumstance. For some, such as Donald Dodds, the beauty of the creatures living in their natural habitat becomes a focus of celebration, and is sufficient reason for conservation and wildlife regulations to protect them. Others, such as Mina Hubbard, are awed by the seemingly numberless sweep of the great animal herds.

Al Pittman deals with a quite different and all too common response to wildlife — that which is manifested in wanton and indescriminate killing.

This unit, while having a unifying theme dealing with wildlife in our environment, is made up of a variety of literary forms. The selection by Donald Dodds is in the form of a short story with an animal as its central character.

Mina Hubbard's is a descriptive essay with some narrative aspects generated from a diary entry. Horwood writes a naturalist's report, while Pittman writes in poetic prose. The selections within the unit are representative of many parts of the province and several chronological periods and writing styles.

Study of this unit should involve the student in a process which will lead to the establishment of personal values in relation to these aspects of the environment. Through reading, thinking and discussion the student should vicariously experience many of the prime emotions of love, joy, triumph, anger and guilt, and come to a more complete self-understanding. This will be enhanced by a critical evaluation of each selection, and analysis of the relationship to other literature. The skills and concepts necessary for cumulative appreciation may be acquired as the selections are brought to the student for study and enjoyment.

A professional wildlife biologist who has spent much time studying living animals in their own habitat would certainly have a great deal of information about his subject. The presentation of that information in an interesting and enjoyable form requires skill in writing as well as in observation. The author of this selection demonstrates skill in both areas. His semi-omniscient approach to the telling of the story allows him a degree of objectivity which is effective in leading the reader to an emotional attachment to the characters. Projection and flashback techniques are used effectively to convey basic information about the period of calving and the way in which the habitat is used. The difference in sensitivity of a moose's hearing as compared to its eyesight is subtly illustrated by different emphasis on sounds as compared to sights in the story. Also notice an occasional shift from past to present tense in order to bring the reader more intimately into the setting.

Alces - the moose

The cow moose moved from the thicket of budding alders lining the river-bank into the shallows and stopped. She turned her head towards the beaver lodge down-stream as the light lap of water from the swimming beaver crept an inch up her sturdy legs, rolled back, then crept up again. For several minutes the movement of water against her leg held her attention in the direction of the beaver lodge. No air stirred on this cool and dusky night. The water had been motionless only moments before. A few hundred yards above the lodge it still mirrored a perfect, darkening image of scattered clouds now salted with starlight.

Algen listened. She recognized delicate sounds as the movements of the beaver but curiosity made her attentive. One of the beavers moved up-stream towards her. With its head breaking the water into a perfect shimmering V, it swam smoothly abreast of the moose as Algen turned slowly to follow the movement. Mamshet stopped swimming and lay quietly watching his audience for a few seconds, then swam on. Algen began to wade slowly deeper into the clear spring river. The snow had only recently abandoned the forests, leaving the world once again to the renewed and the unborn. A week ago, the river still flowed above its banks in many places. Now lowered, nearly to its normal flow, it had left masses of debris along its banks and about the bases of the alders. Early summer rains would mat this debris and great green fronds would combine with slender stems of sedges to mask its ugliness.

Algen began to swim as she moved farther from the littered bank. The strong and steady current eased her downstream and her wake formed an irregular curving bow as it settled below her and disappeared. She headed for an island in the middle of the river, an island no more than 200 yards long and perhaps a hundred yards wide, dense with yew, wild raisin, and mountain maple on the forest floor. A canopy of birch and fir sheltered these plants and a lush fern growth would soon appear in every available opening in the under-story.

As her feet scraped bottom near the island shoreline, Algen raised herself from the water. She stumbled and splashed her feet and legs about for balance before reaching the heavy sand beach. Once on steady, dry footing, she flicked her ears, shook her mane, and wrinkled the heavily haired skin along her back and sides. It was several minutes before she moved slowly into the dense island cover, stopping to bite the tips of a young mountain maple that grew on the lower edge of the sloping water-torn bank.

It was mid-May in the valley of the Upper Humber River. Each spring on or within a day of the twentieth of this month Algen gave birth to a single calf. Like most moose, she never had twins, although she had often seen twin calves with other cows. This year she moved to the calving site as usual and spent six days wandering aimlessly to the shoreline and back to her concealed resting-place, stopping occasionally to feed.

Alces, a lanky, spindly-legged, reddish-brown calf, was born shortly before daybreak. He had large brown eyes, rather long floppy ears, a slight ridge of vertically patterned mane hair, and a tiny, wriggling stub tail, so short that the young moose, like his mother, looked almost incomplete. He was a miniature of his mother except that his head was proportionately shorter and lacked a bell. Beneath Algen's chin and neck hung a wisp of skin covered with longish hair. All adult moose have these bells in varying sizes and shapes. Some hang to the ground, others are heavy, thick, and short. Even Alces had the very early beginnings of such a bell, and, as he grew, the dewlap would develop into a definite shape that would help distinguish him from other moose.

Alces slept a great deal during the first few days of his life. At times his mother would leave him for as long as two or three hours while she foraged for food. When she returned, he would be hungry and would suck until his belly bulged hard.

The place Algen had chosen to calve was in the midst of an extremely thick bed of ground hemlock interspersed with second-growth balsam fir. The yew grew high here on this fertile island, to well over four feet. In this dense coniferous bed Alces was safely hidden from man and beast. Algen was casual in her movements, so that any creature watching would take her to be feeding aimlessly — bent on browsing, nothing more.

When Alces was ten days old he began moving about the island with his mother. As Algen browsed the bursting buds, Alces would pick daintily at many things about the forest floor that to him appeared to be food. When something tasted unpleasant Alces would open his mouth, drop his head, and shake it from side to side as he protruded his tongue to spit the thing out. As his senses sharpened, he no longer made these errors. He grazed on the leaves and shoots of trees, bushes such as mountain maple, wood ferns, and other small plants. At the same time, he still nursed and would continue to nurse until early fall when his mother refused to nurse him any longer.

One day in June, Algen decided to leave the island for the eastern shore of the river. As he had done for nearly every day of his young life, Alces followed his mother about the island during the hour of daybreak, feeding on early green leaves, sedges, and ferns. But instead of going back to one of their resting-places as she usually did, Algen began to move into the water. At first, expecting his mother to return, Alces stood watching from the shore. Algen moved deeper and deeper until only the top of her back and head showed above the surface, then looked back and called softly.

Alces grew excited. He ran and pranced about the shoreline, lifting his forelegs high and stamping them down deliberately. His ears were laid back, almost flat, as he threatened imaginary nothings to his right and his left and on the ground before him. His mother's calls became more frequent and he watched her swim short circles and return to the same point. But Alces only pranced harder and even ran to the woodland cover of the island he now knew so well, circled, and returned — once, twice, three times. At last he stopped near the water's edge and looked towards Algen. Then, slowly, cautiously, retreating several times before moving into the water to his knees, Alces inched towards his waiting mother.

But just as he reached her, the water became too deep! Alces struggled. His front legs flailed about his mother's rump, grasped her tightly about her rear quarters, and then, as he moved his hind legs in a frantic effort to climb to more complete safety, Algen moved into deeper water and began to swim. Alces stopped struggling and hung on tightly with his forelegs. Across the river Algen moved with her calf, carried down-stream slowly as she swam. When she felt earth and stone under her feet she rose up to her height and walked, dumping Alces into water still too deep for him to touch bottom. He was forced to thrash his legs and swim, barely holding his head above water, for a few feet until he, too, reached the safety of dry land.

Many times Algen would repeat this process throughout the ensuing weeks as she swam and fed about the area of aquatic plant growth where the river widened above the island. And soon Alces would swim alone.

One day Alces had been frisking about his mother as they travelled together — charging her, threatening with mighty gestures, waving an antlerless ear-flattened head and showing the whites of his eyes — when their movement brought them to the edge of a river backwater filled with lillies, spatterdock, and pondweeds. Out in the water they fed upon these plants growing in abundance. They had been feeding slowly for several minutes when a great commotion attracted their attention.

Moving through a narrow strait in the backwater, between two encroaching bog formations, came a noisy family of otters. Splashing, diving, and grunting, they churned the water to bubbles along their staggered pathway.

An otter family leads a playful existence. Although they must fish hard for the trout and young salmon that abound in the waters of the Upper Humber River, and forage many hours along the banks and bottom of the shallow channels lining the river here for larvae of aquatic insects, their work is turned into play. The successful otter pup must fight and flee to keep his captured trophy from brother and sister, for what one has the others want.

Algen and Alces had chosen a place to feed only a few feet from an otter rock in this quiet water. Here the otters would climb, their coats at once glistening dry in the morning sunlight, to eat their catches. They struggled with one another greedily for each trout, the victor crunching the head bones quickly down, only partly chewing the remainder of the soft-bodied food. Like others of the weasel family, the otters sometimes closed their eyes while eating, and the knowledge of this trait often meant success to the otter-hunter when the pelts were prime and the market good. Here, however, the otters had little to fear during the spring and summer as they fed, slept, and played about the back-water.

To the otter family, the watching moose were an interesting diversion. Diving and surfacing around the ungainly giants, they grunted and blinked, talking among themselves. They showed no fear and continued to fish between periods of observation.

The trout has little chance of escape from an otter in open water. Swimming in a straight line, the otter easily overtakes the fish. Only as the trout turns can it gain time to live, yet it never turns enough. Its only way of escape is to hide in weed growth.

Alces would soon grow used to seeing and hearing otters by day or night. Yet the thrashing of playful otters at their slides or in the pools was but a small part of Alces' world of sound. As morning broke, the twilight creatures, among them other moose in the backwater, made movement and feeding noises. The water slushed as the moose moved his legs and splattered as it dripped from plants torn from the cozy bottom. Ducks splashed and then broke a silence in the air with the beating of their wings. The early-morning snipe winnowed. Beaver travelled from lodge to lily-beds, the kits daring to travel farther each morning. Muskrats nibbled submerged buds of yellow lillies and trimmed the growing sedges, nourishing themselves to produce their litters. The noises from the actions of each mammal or bird were separate and important and Alces knew them.

The first song-bird of the morning is the whitethroat singing his repetitious, plaintive song. But soon he is joined by the fox-sparrow, the purple finch, the water-thrush. Then the sun begins to dry the crystal webs of morning and warm the air, destroying the mists. The early-morning songs fade and are replaced by the sounds of tree-warblers, wild bees, and ravens.

As evening approaches, the earliest sounds of daylight are often repeated, yet the thrushes, fox-sparrows, and white-throats dominate the bird world, until night envelops the wild land and the dusky noises slowly, gracefully fade to the occasional call of a horned owl, and, always, the forgetful whitethroat.

Alces distinguished all these sounds — and the singing of the wind, the trickling of the brook, the thundering of the waterfall, the snap of a limb, the roll of thunder. And there were others, from fox kits, weasel, and bear, from dying hare, from feeding trout. As the sounds were distinctive to the moose, so were the smells, and, more dimly perhaps than these, the sights.

● ● ●

In Newfoundland the time of warmth moves swiftly, hurriedly, through the season of growth. It is but a moment from bud to fruit....Alces seldom nurse d now, for his mother was refusing him; at first she was only impatient, but now she was almost determined. The cow and calf had long since left the backwater area and had moved a mile away to the woodland second growth following a recent cutting of the pulp-woods by lumbermen. Instead of aquatic plants, which had grown less palatable as summer grew old, the moose now fed upon sedges and woody twigs.

Algen and Alces ranged over a larger area now. During the warmer months they stayed near the backwater, spending much time lying in the wet marshes or standing in the cooling river. Since flies were less troublesome late in the season, they seldom went to the river now. Below them lay a woods road. Lately the two moose had spent much time in the cut-overs bordering this road. Here they fed during the early-morning and sunset hours, resting the remainder of the time, except for occasional nocturnal forays in the more open areas of young fir growth.

● ● ●

Fog weighted the late-summer leaves in the alder-bed. The world was small. No frost had yet weakened this year's green growth, but the ground already carried leaves faded by the summer's daytime heat and cool nights. A light mist penetrated the densest thickets about the alders' edge. The snowshoe rabbit lay huddled in its form, having ventured only to feed on a few birch leaves near by. The forest was soundless. Even the bird life was still this morning, save for the occasional call of a whitethroat that had not yet flown south.

A cow moose lay motionless with her calf, almost in sleep, resting.

He knew where to find the animals and on such a morning it was not difficult to move carefully and surprise them. He was soaking wet but, since there was no air stirring, he was not cold. Slowly the poacher walked along the tiny brook that snaked through the alders. Even when he accidentally broke the giant cow-parsnip, there was no noise this morning. The plant only leaned towards the ground and the sound it made was no louder than the poacher's foot sinking into the grass. When the moose heard the first noise, the intruder was only a hundred feet away. The huge, dim forms rose, and the poacher fired....Alces trotted at once a few yards and stopped, his ears flattened, head high. He looked back at Algen, standing with her neck arched towards the ground. The second report sounded and Algen's lower jaw dropped as if hinged, and waggled loosely. A third thundered through the woodlands. Algen hunched her back and swayed. She spread her legs wide to support her weight. The fourth and fifth reports sounded. Algen folded slowly to the ground.

Alces moved uncertainly in a half-circle, testing the wind. He trotted towards his mother, then retreated.

The poacher sat down and rolled a cigarette, lit it, and took time to smoke it. He was alone. It was very still this morning and not even a jay appeared. His shots seemed dulled to him, yet they were heard by residents a mile away.

He went up to the moose. Expertly he cut open the stomach to the diaphragm, reached down, and cut out the liver. Then he removed the heart. Next he cut the oesophagus and larynx and pulled back, dumping the entrails and paunch to the ground. He took out the kidneys and removed the tongue. Now, with his ax he split the backbone and rib-cage to the neck. His keen-edged knife sliced through the tough neck muscle and the skin, and the head was removed. Working his knife between the vertebrae he disjointed the bone and halved each side. Then he removed each leg at the knee joint.

The poacher smoked another cigarette. He was sweating now from the activity of butchering. When he finished the cigarette he picked up a hind quarter with a rope sling and carried it down to the road a mile away. Here he cached it beneath some branches of slash from the cut-over fir. On the fourth trip he carried his rifle and ax. He picked a small fir standing close to the road and made two blaze marks on it and went home.

Donald Dodds
(from *Wild Captives*)

Donald G. Dodds was born in the United States but has spent most of his adult life in Canada. He was employed as a wildlife biologist by the Newfoundland government and spent many months in the field making observations and studying the inter-relationships of wild creatures in their natural habitat. The writing of his reports and scientific notes and data was augmented by the kind of descriptive creative writing which is found in *Wild Captives*, published in 1965, from which this selection is taken. Since leaving Newfoundland Dr. Dodds has done scientific work for the Canadian government, and also for international agencies in Rome, Kenya, Zambia, Ethiopia, Botswana and Trinidad. He is Professor of Wildlife Management at Acadia University in Nova Scotia.

Questions

1. The story is well advanced before man is introduced. Why has the author chosen to delay the mention of man? What is the effect for the reader?

2. This selection has most of the characteristics of a short story. Which of the elements is dominant? Where is the climax? Why does the author not prolong the climax?

3. The author's treatment of the moose and the poacher seems to be objective. The point of view is remote, detached and objective, yet we sense that the author's sympathies are with the animals. Can you suggest the techniques he used to make this subtle impression?

4. Why does the author choose to make the man a poacher? If the man were a legitimate hunter would the outcome have been different for the moose? Would the story have been the same for you?

5. Foreshadowing is a technique used to build interest in a story's development. Find at least one example of foreshadowing in this story. What is its effect?

Activities

1. Read "An Otter" by Ted Hughes on page 101 of *Theme and Image*. Compare the description in the poem with the description in this selection.

2. Read the first part of "Civil Service Civilities" by Farley Mowat on page 92 of *Man's Search for Values*. How does Mowat's attitude toward wildlife biology compare with that of Dr. Dodds?

3. Suggest a continuation of the story for Alces following the death of Algen. Then read the full selection in *Wild Captives*.

4. Sketch the scene described in the second paragraph of the selection. Sketch one of the scenes described in the paragraphs immediately following Algen's call to Alces from the river. What is your impression of the author's intent after reading these paragraphs?

5. Use source books, such as *Shrubs of Newfoundland* published by the Newfoundland Tourist Department to help you identify yew, wild raisin, mountain maple, spatterdock and cowparsnip. Collect a specimen of each and bring them to class.

6. Find examples of figurative language in the selection. Try to identify precisely what each is, and suggest the author's intention in using it.

7. Read "Vulpes — the fox" in *Passages*, a text used in Grade IX.

8. Read the epilogue of *Wild Captives*. The story as it appears here is an edited version combining the first half of the original and the epilogue of the book itself.

In The Lure of the Labrador Wild, Dillon Wallace gives a graphic account of the failure of the Hubbard expedition in 1903 and the death of its leader, Leonidas Hubbard. In 1905 Mina Hubbard set out with four guides to accomplish what her husband had attempted to do two years before — to be the first to traverse the Labrador peninsula from Lake Melville to Ungava Bay. The account of this successful expedition is contained in her book A Woman's Way Through Unknown Labrador, first published in 1908. That book from which this selection is taken focusses on four major topics: the importance of completing the journey and thus fulfilling a beloved husband's dream. The physical journey through interesting and formerly unknown territory, the relationships which developed between the members of the expedition, especially that between Mina and George Elson, the lead guide, and the beautiful and sensitive descriptions of the terrain, rivers, lakes, sky and wildlife. The latter theme dominates the selection included here. Mina Hubbard's reaction to the mass of the moving herd and her response to individual creatures reveals the sensitivity and compassion of this refined and seemingly delicate woman who finds herself in the midst of the Labrador wilderness, north and west of Lake Michikamaw.

The selection comprises most of Chapter Thirteen of A Woman's Way Through Unknown Labrador. The incidents described are set in the height of land north of Lake Michikamaw and Lake Michikamats, just south of the upper George River. Even at that time the herd was only a fraction of its former size due to "unreasoning slaughter" and "fires...destroying the moss on which they feed." Mrs. Hubbard's written and photographic information was the first accurate data to be obtained about this herd.

Students should note in this account the revelation of the personality of the writer in almost every event and incident described, and the conversational tone of the writing. These are marks of a good essay and Mrs. Hubbard uses this form to convey her impressions on witnessing a unique event.

The Migrating Caribou

Tuesday morning, August 8th, dawned clear and calm, and Gilbert came forth to light the fire, singing: "Glory, glory, hallelujah! as we go marching along." Yet before the tents were taken down the wind had sprung up from the southwest, and it was with difficulty that the canoes were launched and loaded.

A short distance above our starting-point, we were obliged to run into a sheltered bay, where part of the load was put ashore, and with the canoes thus lightened we crossed to a long, narrow point which reached half-way across from the other side, making an excellent breakwater between the upper and lower parts of the lake. The crossing was accomplished in safety, though it was rough enough to be interesting, and Job and Joe went back for what had been left behind.

The point terminated in a low, pebbly beach, but its banks further up were ten to twelve feet high, and above it was covered with reindeer moss. Towards the outer end there were thickets of dwarf spruce, and throughout its length scattered trees that had bravely held their heads up in spite of the storms of the dread northern winter. To the south of the point was a beautiful little bay, and at its head a high sand mound which we found to be an Indian burying-place. There were four graves, one large one with three little ones at its foot, each surrounded by a neatly made paling, while a wooden cross, bearing an inscription in Montagnais, was planted at the head of each moss-covered mound. The inscriptions were worn and old except that on one of the little graves. Here the cross was a new one, and the palings freshly made. Some distance out on the point stood a skeleton wigwam carpeted with boughs that were still green, and lying about outside were the fresh cut shavings telling where the Indian had fashioned the new cross and the enclosure about the grave of his little one. Back of this solitary resting-place were the moss-covered hills with their sombre forests, and as we turned from them we looked out over the bay at our feet, the shining waters of the lake, and beyond it to the blue, round-topped hills reaching upward to blend with exquisite harmony into the blue and silver of the great dome that stooped to meet them. Who could doubt that romance and poetry dwell in the heart of the Indian who chose this for the resting-place of his dead.

Walking back along the point we found it cut by caribou trails, and everywhere the moss was torn and trampled in a way that indicated the presence there of many of the animals but a short time since. Yet it did not occur to me that we might possibly be on the out-skirts of the march of the migrating caribou. Ptarmigan were there in numbers, and flew up all along our way. We passed a number of old camps, one a large oblong, sixteen feet in length, with two fireplaces in it, each marked by a ring of small rocks, and a doorway at either end. Near where we landed, close in the shelter of a thicket of dwarf spruce, was a deep bed of boughs, still green, where some wandering aboriginal had spent the night without taking time or trouble to erect his wigwam, and who in passing on had set up three poles pointing northward to tell his message to whoever might come after.

The wind continued high, and squalls and heavy showers passed. Nevertheless, when lunch was over we pushed on, keeping close to the west shore of the lake. Little more than a mile further up the men caught sight of deer feeding not far from the water's edge. We landed, and climbing to the top of the rock wall saw a herd of fifteen or more feeding in the swamp. I watched them almost breathless. They were very beautiful to me. Soon they saw us and trotted off into the bush, though without sign of any great alarm. George and Job made off across the swamp to the right to investigate, and not long after returned, their eyes blazing with excitement,

126

to say that there were hundreds of them not far away.

Slipping hurriedly back into the canoes we paddled rapidly and silently to near the edge of the swamp. Beyond it was a barren hill, which from near its foot sloped more gradually to the water. Along the bank, where this lower slope dropped to the swamp, lay a number of stags, with antlers so immense that I wondered how they could possibly carry them. Beyond, the lower slope of the hill seemed to be a solid mass of caribou, while its steeper part was dotted over with many feeding on the luxuriant moss.

Those lying along the bank got up at the sight of us, and withdrew towards the great herd in rather leisurely manner, stopping now and then to watch us curiously. When the herd was reached, and the alarm given, the stags lined themselves up in the front rank and stood facing us, with heads high and a rather defiant air. It was a magnificent sight. They were in summer garb of pretty brown, shading to light grey and white on the under parts. The horns were in velvet, and those of the stags seemed as if they must surely weigh down the heads on which they rested. It was a mixed company, for male and female were already herding together. I started towards the herd, kodak in hand, accompanied by George, while the others remained at the shore. The splendid creatures seemed to grow taller as we approached, and when we were within two hundred and fifty yards of them their defiance took definite form, and with determined step they came towards us.

The sight of that advancing army under such leadership, was decidedly impressive, recalling vivid mental pictures made by tales of the stampeding wild cattle in the west. It made one feel like getting back to the canoe, and that is what we did. As we ran toward the other men I noticed a peculiar smile on their faces, which had in it a touch of superiority. I understood in part when I turned, for the caribou had stopped their advance, and were again standing watching us. Now the others started towards the herd. Emboldened by their courage, and thinking that perhaps they held the charm that would make a close approach to the herd possible, I accompanied them. Strange to relate it was but a few minutes till we were all getting back to the canoes, and we did not again attempt to brave their battle front. We and the caribou stood watching each other for some time. Then the caribou began to run from either extreme of the herd, some round the south end of the hill and the others away to the north, the line of stags still maintaining their position.

After watching them for some time we again entered the canoes. A short paddle carried us round the point beyond which the lake bent to the north-west, and there we saw them swimming across the lake. Three-quarters of a mile out was an island, a barren ridge standing out of the water, and from mainland to island they formed as they swam a broad unbroken bridge; from the farther end of which they poured in steady stream over the hill-top, their flying forms clearly outlined against the sky. How long we watched them I could not say, for I was too excited to take any note of time; but finally the main body had passed.

Yet when we landed above the point from which they had crossed, companies of them, eight, ten, fifteen, twenty in a herd, were to be seen in all directions. When I reached the top of the ridge accompanied by George

127

and Gilbert, Job and Joe were already out on the next hill beyond, and Job was driving one band of a dozen or more toward the water at the foot of the hill, where some had just plunged in to swim across. Eager to secure a photo or two at closer range than any I had yet obtained, I handed George my kodak and started down the hill at a pace which threatened every second to be too fast for my feet, which were not dressed in the most appropriate running wear. However the foot of the hill was reached in safety. There a bog lay across our way. I succeeded in keeping dry for a few steps, then gave it up and splashed through at top speed. We had just hidden ourselves behind a huge boulder to wait for the coming of the herd, when turning round I saw it upon the hill from which we had just come. While exclaiming over my disappointment I was startled by a sound immediately behind me, and turning saw a splendid stag and three does not twenty feet away. They saw us and turned, and I had scarcely caught my breath after the surprise when they were many more than twenty feet away, and there was barely time to snap my shutter on them before they disappeared over the brow of the hill.

The country was literally alive with the beautiful creatures, and they did not seem to be much frightened. They apparently wanted only to keep what seemed to them a safe distance between us, and would stop to watch us curiously within easy rifle shot. Yet I am glad I can record that not a shot was fired at them. Gilbert was wild, for he had in him the hunter's instinct in fullest measure. The trigger of Job's rifle clicked longingly, but they never forgot that starvation broods over Labrador, and that the animal they longed to shoot might some time save the life of one in just such extremity as that reached by Mr. Hubbard and his party two years before.

The enjoyment of the men showed itself in the kindling eyes and faces luminous with pleasure. All his long wilderness experience had never afforded Job anything to compare with that which this day had brought him. He was like a boy in his abandon of delight, and I am sure that if the caribou had worn tails we should have seen Job running over the hills holding fast to one of them.

Before proceeding farther we re-ascended the hill which we first climbed to take a look at the lake. It could be seen almost from end to end. The lower part which we had passed was clear, but above us the lake was a network of islands and water. The hills on either side seemed to taper off to nothing in the north, and I could see where the land appeared to drop away beyond this northern horizon which looked too near to be natural. North of Michikamats were more taller lakes, and George showed me our probable route to look for "my river". Squalls and showers had been passing all the afternoon, and as it drew towards evening fragments of rainbow could be seen out on the lake or far away on the hills beyond it. Labrador is a land of rainbows and rainbow colours, and nowhere have I ever seen them so brilliant, so frequent and so variedly manifested. Now the most brilliant one of all appeared close to us, its end resting directly on a rock near the foot of the hill. George never knew before that there is a pot of gold at the end of the rainbow. I suspect he does not believe it yet for I could not persuade him to run to get it. Gilbert, more credulous, made a determined attempt to secure the treasure, but before he reached the rock the rainbow had moved off and carried the gold to the middle of the lake.

Camp was made a little farther up. When it was ready for the night Job and Joe were again off to watch the caribou. They were feeding on the hills and swimming back and forth from island to mainland, now in companies, now a single caribou. Job was so near one as he came out of the water that he could have caught him by the horns. Now and then a distant shout told that Job and the caribou had come to close quarters.

While George and Gilbert prepared supper, I sat writing in my diary with feet stretched to the fire, for I was wet and it was cold that night. Suddenly I was startled to hear George exclaim in tragic tones: "Oh! look there! Isn't that too bad!"

Looking up quickly to see what was the trouble I saw him gazing regretfully at a salt shaker which he had just drawn from his pocket.

"Just see," he exclaimed, "what I've been carrying round in my pocket all the time you were running after those caribou, and never thought about it at all. Well, I am sorry for that. I could just have given you a bit and you would have been all right."

For fifty miles of our journey beyond this point we saw companies of the caribou every day, and sometimes many times a day, though we did not again see them in such numbers. The country was a network of their trails, in the woodlands and bogs cut deep into the soft soil, on the barren hillsides broad, dark bands converging to the crossing place at the river.

At the time I made my journey the general movewment of the caribou was towards the east; but where they had come from or whither they were going we could not tell. Piles of white hair which we found later at a deserted camp on Cabot Lake where the Indians had dressed the skins, and the bank of white hair clinging to the west bank of the George River, opposite our camp of August 15th, four feet above the then water-level, pointed to an earlier occupation of the country, while the deep cut trails and long piles of whitened antlers, found at intervals along the upper George River, all indicated that this country is favourite ground with them. Yet whether they had been continuously in this territory since the spring months or not I did not ascertain. The Indians whom we found at Resolution Lake knew nothing of their presence so near them.

Towards the end of August the following year Mr. Cabot, while on a trip inland from Davis Inlet, on the east coast, found the caribou in numbers along the Height of Land, and when he joined the Indians there, though the great herd had passed, they had killed near a thousand. It would therefore seem not improbable that at the time I made my journey they were bending their steps in the direction of the highlands between the Atlantic and the George.

The movements of the barren ground caribou of Labrador have never been observed in the interior as they have been in the country west of Hudson Bay. So far as I can learn I alone, save the Indians, have witnessed the great migration there.

Mina Hubbard

(from *A Woman's Way Through Unknown Labrador*)

Mina Benson was born in 1870 near Bewdley, Ontario. On January 29th, 1900, she married Leonidas Hubbard and moved to the United States. In January of 1904 she received word that her husband had died in the Labrador wilderness, and for some time she was grief-stricken. She eventually came to blame Dillon Wallace, her husband's friend, for his death. When Wallace decided to complete the journey in 1905, Mina Hubbard determined that she would complete it first. Her successful expedition led to recognition for her by geographical societies and biologists on both sides of the Atlantic, and her book was an outstanding success. In 1908 she married an English Member of Parliament and did not return to Canada until the 1930's. She died in an accident at the age of 86.

Questions

1. Mina Hubbard's background and way of life are quite different from those of her guides and the Indian who has just buried his child on the sandy point. What do you think of her response to this sad event? In what other way might she have responded.

2. Is Mrs. Hubbard in control of this expedition, or is she simply a "passenger" being transported across the country? Find evidence for your answer in the selection.

3. This account is written in a chronological style, which could easily become boring. What techniques and devices of language and style does Mrs. Hubbard use to maintain the reader's interest?

4. Which details in the account work together to suggest the size of the herd? Which details make the herd seem particularly alive? Which details of movement lend an air of reality to the whole scene?

5. What contributes to the tension in this selection? What is the response of the animals to this tension? What is the response of the people?

6. Mina asks George to find the gold at the rainbow's end, and later he suggests that she could have caught a caribou by

shaking salt on its tail. What does this suggest to you about their relationship? What is your response to this?

7. What would be the effect of changing the purpose of the expedition from observation to hunting?

Activities

1. Find one example of intense action and frenzied movement combined with deep emotion, all described in one or two sentences. How does the author accomplish this without drawing our attention away from the scene itself?

2. Mrs. Hubbard uses much figurative language and some poetic devices in this account. Try to find at least one example of metaphor, simile, alliteration and personification. Discuss your findings with others in your class.

3. Read "Keep Your Own Things" by Irene Baird on page 66 of *Man's Search for Values*. Can you find indications in "The Migrating Caribou" that the advice given by Irene Baird would eventually be necessary for the native people of Labrador?

4. Compare the imaginary response of the Beothuck on pages 71-72 of *Riverrun* by Peter Such with that of Mrs. Hubbard in this selection. Discuss this comparison and the different settings with your teacher or others in your class.

5. Compare the attitudes of Mina Hubbard and Donald Dodds toward the wildlife they observe.

6. Sketch one of the scenes described in the third paragraph of the selection. Write an appropriate caption for your drawing.

7. Mrs. Hubbard describes the movement of the caribou from the land to an island in the lake. Sketch this scene as you think she might have seen it from her canoe.

No life exists in isolation; every living thing supports, and is supported by, other living things. The chain has one end in the microscopic world and the other represented by the largest living creatures. Nowhere is this more apparent than in the oceans. Nowhere in the oceans is it more apparent than off the coast of Newfoundland. Harold Horwood chooses one of the most astounding aspects of this phenomena of nature to amaze us, and to locate man in the chain. In this selection the miracle of the caplin is the centrepiece of the panorama of life described by a writer who has spent much of his time studying nature. The caplin scull, a commonplace happening for us, takes on new and wonderful significance as we see it not simply as an event which recurs annually, but as part of the whole world of marine life.

The Miracle of the Caplin

All along the east coast of Newfoundland, summer begins with the Caplin Scull. At Outer Cove and Middle Cove, at Torbay and Beachy Cove, at Northern Bay and Spillers Cove, as June begins to mellow toward July men slip down to cliffs and beaches every day at dawn to inspect the landwash and the green waters heaving restlessly beyond. Then one morning word runs like wildfire through the villages, "The caplin are in!"

An explosion of activity follows, as everyone makes for the sloping ridges of sand and gravel, men with cast nets, some also with horses and carts or beach sleds, boys with bar nets and dip nets, women with buckets and washing tubs, even people from the city with saucepans and colanders. They all go to reap the incredible harvest of the caplin, small silver fish that pour ashore in billions for a week, so plentiful that you can often catch them with shovels, or load a truck in half an hour with the help of a simple cast net.

The oceans off Newfoundland are one of the world's richest feeding grounds for fish. Here, where the Gulf Stream meets the Labrador Current there is a terrific growth of animal and vegetable plankton. Feeding on these riches, thousands of millions of the most prolific food fish reach maturity every year — none more numerous than the seven-inch caplin (pronounced *cay*-plin), dark green and silver and irridescent, and shaped like slender torpedoes.

As the water warms, and sunlight filters down through the shallow sea, chemical changes in their bodies set off powerful instincts that drive the caplin relentlessly toward shore — toward fulfillment of their life cycle, toward death and renewal. For many will never reach the spawning beaches, and most of those that do will never return to sea. Only a few will ever again reach the indigo depths from which they now rise toward the shallow, sun-washed in-shore waters. In vast numbers they stream past the headlands, past Cape St. Francis and Cape Bonavista and Cape Baccalieu, into the bays, and on toward the sand and shingle beaches, compressed ever more and more into dense schools that darken the water, obscure the bottom, and can even slow a power boat that plunges through the living mass of small bodies.

This is the Caplin Scull, the annual miracle that renews the Newfoundland fisheries and makes them the most productive in the world.

For as the caplin crowd toward shore, everything else in the sea follows along behind: big sharks and small flatfish, mighty whales and foot-long squid in vast shoals — a regular nature parade. The whales come dancing over the water, tossing their heads and shaking their tails as if in play. The squid come pulsing through the shallows, moving backwards by jet propulsion. Both feed upon the caplin until they are glutted. Millions of little fish are scooped into the following jaws, some singly, some in bucketfuls. But they close their ranks, moving in tight formations, and continue without deviation toward shore.

Most important of the many creatures following the caplin are the enormous masses of cod. This fish, which was the basis of the Newfoundland economy for half a millenium, is drawn toward shore by the caplin, and so arrives at the trap berths where it can be taken by the millions in the traps and the cod seines. Landings of cod in Newfoundland run into the hundreds of millions of pounds annually. They are most plentiful while the Caplin Scull is on, though many remain throughout the summer, feeding on other small fish that come to shore in their turn. A few part-time fishermen who put briefly to sea when the caplin arrive are spoken of contemptuously by the full-timers as 'fishing only in the Caplin Scull'.

But when the caplin first arrive even the hardened cod-fisherman is likely to neglect his net loft in favour of a few hours on the beach, working amid the explosive violence that he finds there. The caplin blacken the water of the coves, often in a solid mass from headland to headland. They crowd the beaches, and if the surf is at all heavy, are rolled up on the shore in great waves, stranded, and left to die by the retreating tide. These windrows of caplin are sometimes three feet deep and a quarter of a mile long.

The cast net is a circular mesh, seven or eight feet in diameter when fully spread, edged with leaden balls and fitted with drawstrings that close it like a purse. I have often landed more caplin that I could carry with a single throw of the net, and I once filled a jeep and a motorboat in less than an hour at Beachy Cove. Bar nets will catch even more. Taken out by a boat to enclose a section of the swarming caplin, the bar net is then drawn toward shore, or 'dried up' like a cod trap, until the fish can be dipped out of it with brailers. Ten tons or so are often taken in a single haul, and a large bar net can take a hundred tons or more.

Though most Newfoundlanders love to eat caplin, either fresh, corned, or smoked, only a very small part of the total catch goes directly for food. Some millions of the little fish are used to catch larger fish on baited trawl-lines, and are frozen by the public bait depots to be sold back to the fishermen in fall and winter when bait fish are scarce. Some are put into pits and covered with sod or topsoil to rot down to compost, and are mixed with rotted peat or straw for fertilizer. Thousands upon thousands of tons of caplin are spread directly on hayfields, dug into potato gardens, or buried around the roots of rhubarb and cabbage plants, where they quickly turn to raw fish manure. The Newfoundland soil, in most east-coast outports, is not very fertile, but such fertility as it can boast is largely due to fishermen spreading caplin upon it for the past three or four hundred years.

A beach party with a caplin fry — a thousand or so of the little fish, fresh out of the sea, cooked until they crackle, and washed down with generous draughts of Demerara rum — is a real Newfoundland event. In these circumstances, the odour of sizzling fish mixing with the wood smoke, and salt air to quicken the appetite, some people have been known to eat a hundred caplin at a sitting.

Many outport families put away a barrel of corned caplin — lightly salted and sun dried — for the winter, and some make an extra barrel for their dogs. These cured fish need only two or three minutes cooking in a frying pan or a hot oven. They are smoked not only in smoke houses or smokers improvised out of barrels or puncheons, but even in the tops of chimneys, with green spruce boughs in the stove to produce plenty of aromatic smoke. But the best smoking mixture includes blackberry bushes, peat, and wood chips.

The sex life of the caplin, which starts this whole chain of activity, is a weird and wonderful thing. To begin with, nature plays a mean trick by keeping the sexes segregated. Swarms of lonely bachelors packed densely together arrive at the spawning beaches and mill about in utter confusion, wondering where all the ladies are. At a few beaches, the females may never show up at all, to the great delight of the caplin catchers, who regard the larger, meatier male fish as the only one fit to grace a plate. Even at beaches where the girls put in a belated appearance, their consorts usually arrive several days ahead of them, and die by the millions without the solace of a female fin.

But when the sexes do manage to keep an assignation there is frolic such as few fish enjoy. The caplin are quite unlike their larger cousins, those puritans of the animal kingdom who mate only by correspondence, without bodily contact. They not only enjoy physical courtship — they mate in *threes* rather than in pairs. The males have special little hooks on their fins designed for the sole purpose of seizing females. They have ridges along their sides for holding her firmly in place. Two of them capture a single female, and conduct her, struggling, to the beach. There, between high and low tide, in water an inch or so deep, they line her up between them, and she deposits her golden spawn while they emit clouds of fertilizing milt. When breeding is at its peak, the water becomes cloudy with milt and the foreshore spongy with spawn. The tiny eggs surround and encrust each pebble or grain of gravel, so that the whole beach becomes springy, like a carpet, as you walk along the shore.

The Caplin Scull is not just a phenomenon of nature, but also a period of the year, and even a special kind of weather — 'mausy' weather, with high humidity, frequent fogs or drizzles, easterly winds; Caplin Scull weather has so long been associated with full cod traps that some fishermen are willing to swear that easterly winds and light rains bring the fish to the land.

The furious activity of the Caplin Scull lasts from about the middle of June to the middle of July, for the caplin strike in at slightly different times on different beaches. For those few weeks all the fish plants work overtime, taking boatloads of fish from the inshore fishermen, sometimes round, but usually 'gutted head on', fresh from the knives, and often cleaned on board the boats as they come in from the trap berths. You can always tell a boat on which they are cleaning the fish as they come to shore by the flock of gulls that follows it, rising and dipping, feasting on the offal that is thrown over the stern.

The fish are filleted, frozen, and packaged, some frozen into large blocks to be made into fish sticks. The fishermen themselves work an eighteen-hour day, but even working around the clock the plants are often unable to handle the glut. They then turn away whole boatloads of fish, which must be split and put into salt, or occasionally dumped back into the ocean, for the Caplin Scull is a season of great plenty, even, occasionally, of excess. It is not unusual for a small open trap skiff, powered by a single cylinder gasoline engine, to land 30,000 pounds of fish daily while the caplin are in.

Those who have time for sport can find plenty of it on the caplin beaches or in the waters just off shore. Among the fish that follow the caplin right to the rocks are perch and sole, both of which are very easily taken with baited trout hooks or light spinning rods. Casting from shore between the shoals of caplin, an angler canm easily land in an hour more sole than he can carry. The fishing is fast, and you never can tell what you may hook around the edges of a swarm of caplin.

Those who like to get down where they can meet the fish eye to eye have also learned that the Caplin Scull is a happy hunting-ground. Skin-divers and spear-fishermen, chasing the fish that chase the caplin, find them so plentiful that they soon become choosey, and take only the largest specimens. It is reasonably safe sport, too, for no dangerous fish are known to frequent Newfoundland waters regularly. The only large, common sharks are the enormous Greenland basking sharks, plankton eaters that never attack swimmers. The scuba-diver's greatest hazards are the chances that he will be beaned by the lead balls of a cast net or hooked by some small boy who is fishing for perch from a headland rock with a trout pole.

Then, one morning, there is silence along the beaches. Three weeks after the miracle of the Caplin Scull begins, it is over, though there may still be caplin for a week or so in other coves to the north or south. Without the myriads of tumbling fish that one had come to expect, the surf, breaking on the foreshore, looks strangely empty. The sand or gravel is coloured with the golden spawn. But that, too, will vanish within a few days. It will hatch into uncountable numbers of minute larval caplin....

• • •

And then, one day, a spring tide comes in, following the track of the full moon, creeping higher than any caplin could reach, beyond the line of the surf, washing the sand, the pebbles, the water-worn boulders, then retreating, past the line of the kelp, along the off-shore shallows. When dawn breaks again the beach lies clean and empty and scoured, as though the Caplin Scull had never been.

Harold Horwood
(from *Newfoundland*)

A biographical note on the author appears on page 71.

Questions

1. In what way does Horwood's style enhance the description of the caplin scull? In your answer make reference to at least two outstanding aspects of the writing style used.

2. What does the meeting of the Gulf Stream and the Labrador current have to do with the abundance of fish?

3. How does Horwood make sure that the reader understands the social importance of the caplin scull in Newfoundland?

Activities

1. Research the current status of caplin stocks and make a statement expressing your opinion of their management.

2. Try to find out if there is any other part of the world where a caplin scull, or something similar, happens.

3. Describe and/or sketch a cast net, a bar net, and a dip net.

4. Draw a sketch map to show the currents and areas mentioned.

5. Compose a song, poem, or music which would be appropriate to accompany a video of the activity of the caplin scull.

This vignette of poetic prose by Al Pittman concerns the destructive instincts in man, here represented by two boys — preoccupied in their activity of killing fish. While out walking the poet witnesses the boys in their apparently senseless activity of killing and begins to question them on why they do what they are doing. Their responses leave him bewildered.

You too must be bewildered by similar experiences in your life. Think as you read this piece of the broader significance of the work. Consider your own instincts to create and to destroy. Why are you on some occasions dominated by one or the other? What are the effects derived from submission to creativity or destruction.

Notes To No One

Walking the beach, taking pleasure in the wind, I come upon two boys with spears. They are following the flatfish as they move along the shore out of the bay into the river's mouth.

Every few minutes they strike, bringing the fish up wiggling on the spiked heads of their homemade weapons. To get them off, they stand on them, pull the spears out with bits of fish flesh on the barbs, and go on, leaving each fish to flap patterns of his death in the windswept sand.

"Why do you do that?", I ask.
"Because," he replies.
"Do you eat them?"
"No."
"Do anything with them?"
"No."
"Then why do you do it?"
"Because they're no good for nothing."
"Just flatfish," the other one says.
"And besides, it's fun."

They pass on up the shore and leave me standing bewildered in my thirtieth year.

Down the beach the boys are singing. Sometimes it is hard to tell their voices from the sound the wind is making.

Al Pittman
(from *Through One More Window*)

A biographical note on the author is to be found on page 83.

Questions

1. What does the author mean by "taking pleasure in the wind"? Is that pleasure still there in the last line? What is in the wind, now?

2. What attitude is reflected by the boys' answer "Just flatfish"? Is this a common attitude? Could that attitude allow a person to say "Just dogs", or "Just moose", or "Just old people"?

3. Do the boys have reasons for doing what they are doing? Comment on the responses given by the boys to the author's questions.

4. Why does the author say he is left "bewildered in my thirtieth year."?

5. What is the significance of the statement "...it is hard to tell their voices from the sound the wind is making"?

6. How would Mina Hubbard have reacted had she, instead of Mr. Pittman, encountered those boys? What would have been the reaction of Donald Dodds? What would have been your reaction?

Activities

1. Read "The Death of a Salmon" by Roderick Haig-Brown, on page 215 of *Writer's Workshop*. Is this mass death different from the slaughter of the flatfish by the boys? If so, how is it different?

2. Read "The Slaughter of the Esquimaux" by Samuel Hearne on page 149 of *Man's Search for Values*. How is the attitude expressed by the Indians similar to the attitude of the two boys? Is there any basic difference? If you think there is, try to express it.

3. Sketch the scene described in the second paragraph. Write a suitable caption.

4. Discuss with your classmates selected topics related to the ease with which killing can become an accepted action, for example, the killing of codfish, or rabbits. Perhaps some examples of killing in war, if discussed from the point of view of why they took place, would throw some light on Mr. Pittman's theme.

AUTHOR INDEX — UNITS 1-4

UNITS 1-4

Bibliography

BIBLIOGRAPHY

A Part of All That We Have Met

Books

Brown, Cassie. *A Winter's Tale*. Toronto: Doubleday, 1976.

Brown, Cassie. *Death on the Ice*. Toronto: Doubleday, 1976.

Brown, Cassie. *Standing Into Danger*. Toronto: Doubleday, 1979.

Cranford, G., and Hillier, R. *Potheads and Drumhoops*. St. John's: Harry Cuff Publications, 1983.

Guy, Ray. *That Far Greater Bay*. St. John's: Breakwater, 1976.

Kent, Rockwell. *North by East*. Connecticut: Wesleyan University Press, 1978.

Poole, C.F. *In Search of the Newfoundland Soul*. St. John's, Harry Cuff Publications, 1982.

Roberts, Dr. Harry. *Newfoundland Fish Boxes*. Fredericton: Brunswick Press, 1982.

Scammell, Arthur. *My Newfoundland*. Montreal: Harvest House, 1966.

Watts, Enos. *After the Locusts*. St. John's: Breakwater, 1974.

Periodicals

Decks Awash. Vol. 10, No. 3, June, 1981. (Shipwrecks between Cape Race and Cape English.)

Decks Awash. Vol. 13, No. 1, January-February, 1984 (Attitudes towards wildlife) (Shipwrecks).

Newfoundland Quarterly. "Simplicity and Survival" by Shane O'Dea. Vol. LXXVIII, No. 3, Fall 1982.

Newfoundland Quarterly. "No Isles of Tranquility" by Ray Guy. Vol. LXXVIII, No. 4, Spring 1983.

Newfoundland Quarterly. "The Return of the Native" by Jessie Mifflin. Vol. LXXIX, No. 4, Spring 1984.

Recordings

Byrne, P.A. and Byrne, I.J. "Towards the Sunset". St. John's: Pigeon Inlet Productions.

Russell, Ted. "Tales From Pigeon Inlet". St. John's: Pigeon Inlet Productions.

Russell, Ted. "The Chronicles of Uncle Mose". St. John's: Pigeon Inlet Productions.

Ocean & Outport

Books

Feather, Jean Hayes. *Sawtooth Harbour Bay*. Don Mills: Thomas Nelson and Sons, 1973.

Fon Eisen, Anthony. *Storm: Dog of Newfoundland*. New York: Charles Scribner's Sons, 1948.

Kipling, Rudyard. *Captains Courageous*. Toronto: Macmillan, 1939.

Duley, Margaret. "Glimpses into Local Literature". *Atlantic Guardian*, July, 1956.

Horwood, Harold. *Newfoundland*. Toronto: MacMillan, 1969.

Memorial University. "Newfoundland Resettlement". St. John's: Memorial University Printing Services, 1978.

Scammell, Arthur. *My Newfoundland*. Montreal: Harvest House, 1966.

Smallwood, J.R. *The Book of Newfoundland*. Volumes I-VI, St. John's: Newfoundland Book Publishers, 1967-1975.

Sparkes, Stanley. "Newfoundlandia in the Classroom". *The Newfoundland Teachers' Association Journal*. St. John's, 1970.

Films

"The Baymen", "The Sea Got In Your Blood", "The Winds of Fogo", National Film Board of Canada.

Introspection

Books

Bartlett, Robert. *Sails Over Ice*. New York: Charles Scribner's Sons, 1934.

Bennet, C.L., and Pierce, Lorne. *Argosy to Adventure*. Toronto: Macmillan of Canada, 1950.

Buitenhuis, Peter. *Selected Poems of E.J. Pratt*. Toronto: Macmillan of Canada, 1968.

Charlesworth, Robert A., and Lee, Dennis. *An Anthology of Verse*. Toronto: Oxford University Press, 1964.

Fogwill, Irving. *A Short Distance Only*. St. John's: Harry Cuff Publications, 1981.

Fowler, A., and Pittman, A. *31 Newfoundland Poets*. St. John's: Breakwater, 1969.

Roberts, Dr. Harry D. *The Newfoundland Fish Boxes*. Fredericton: Brunswick Press, 1982.

Tillotson, G., et al. *Eighteeth-Century English Literature*. New York: Harcourt, Brace and World, 1969.

Watts, Enos. *After the Locusts*. St. John's: Breakwater, 1974.

Refer to any version of The Bible.

Recordings

Walsh, Des. *Newfoundland Poets*. St. John's: Pigeon Inlet Productions.

Wildlife & People

Books

Brooks, William. *Wildlife of Canada*. Toronto: Houslow Press, 1979.

Department of Tourism. *Shrubs of Newfoundland*. St. John's: Province of Newfoundland, March, 1978.

Dodds, Donald. *Wild Captives*. Toronto: Macmillan of Canada, 1965.

Henriksen, Georg. *Hunters In The Barrens*. St. John's: Memorial University of Newfoundland, 1973.

Horwood, Harold. *Newfoundland*. Toronto: Macmillan, 1969.

Hubbard, Mina. *A Woman's Way Through Unknown Labrador*. St. John's: Breakwater, 1981.

Pittman, Al. *Through One More Window*. St. John's: Breakwater, 1974.

Printed in Canada

g